Italian Cooking

Alex Barker

Macdonald Guidelines

Managing editor
Chester Fisher
Series editor
Jim Miles
Editor
Sue Moore
Designer
Robert Wheeler
Picture research
Jenny de Gex
Production
Penny Kitchenham

First published 1979
Macdonald Educational Ltd,
Holywell House, Worship Street,
London EC2A 2EN

Printed and bound by
Waterlow (Dunstable) Ltd

ISBN 0 356 06039 X
(paperback edition)

ISBN 0 356 06439 5
(cased edition)

Contents

The first European cuisine

The tradition of Italian cookery goes back thousands of years: indeed, it was the Italians who in many ways taught the French themselves to cook, and so, indirectly, much of the rest of the world.

History has told us many stories of the gargantuan banquets of the Roman emperors: how peacocks, herons and other birds were delicacies decorated for the table in their own plumage, and how men would eat a whole sheep or pig in one meal. No doubt some of this was true, but only for the very few. For other people the gastronomic facts of life were very different. Records tell us that one staple food was a ground cereal boiled with water and eaten dried like a heavy cake or biscuit. Today this dish is known as *polenta,* and is still cooked in much the same way as in Roman times.

The Romans also made many types of cheese and wine. They developed recipes for foods including gnocchi and cheesecake, both of which are still an important part of the Italian diet, and they grew and imported many herbs and spices.

The rebirth of Italian cooking

Following the fall of the Empire, the excesses of Roman eating disappeared too, and several centuries elapsed before the influence of Eastern countries, encouraged by a renewal of trade, began to have an effect on the way of life in Italy. In time the Italians learnt the Arabian art of making delicate pastries and sweet dishes; they began cultivating sugar for the first time in Europe; and they rediscovered many herbs and spices. By the thirteenth century they were in the habit of eating a form of pasta, introduced from the East – in particular from China.

With the Renaissance a renewed interest made itself felt in cooking as an art. At about this time the first cookery book was published, in Venice, based partly on the notes of the Roman gourmet, Apicius. It brought about many new fashions in eating, one of them being the consumption of sweet things at the beginning of a meal, in particular the Italian favourite of Parma ham with melon or figs.

As the country's wealth spread more evenly and the welfare of the poorer classes improved, the family diet became much as it is today. Pasta played an important part, becoming the basis of much Italian cuisine; and following the introduction of coffee, coffee houses sprang up throughout the country. Among other novelties were vegetables such as peppers and tomatoes, which were grown in many parts of Italy and eventually became essential to its cuisine.

In the course of their evolution the traditions of Italian cooking were exported to France and there developed further. In 1533 Catherine de Medici went to France to marry the future Henri II. Her retinue included skilled cooks, to produce the best Italian food; and in due course the native cooks employed by the court of France discovered the refinements of Italian vegetable cooking; the art of making delicious pastries and sweet dishes with the new

▶ A painting by Zavattari, illustrating the magnificence of an Italian wedding feast. It is entitled 'The Wedding Feast of Teolinda E. Agilulso'. It hangs in the Monza Cathedral.

▲ An ancient Roman mozaic from Pompeii, showing several species of fish still caught for food off the coasts of Italy.

ingredient, sugar; and of course Italian ices. Under Italian influence the French took to eating truffles, and they also adopted the use of the double saucepan comprising one vessel within another and used for heating food slowly. This device was created by a lady called Maria, hence its Italian name of *bagno maria*, rendered into French as *bain-marie*.

A modern cuisine

Notwithstanding its international popularity, Italian food today is far more exciting than Italian restaurants in other countries generally lead us to believe. Every region has produced a soup that is thick, almost like a meal in a bowl, or thin, clear, well-flavoured broths served with shapes of pasta. There are hundreds of brightly coloured, hot or cold antipasti which combine the most exciting of flavours. And there are so many shapes of pasta – originating either from place names or nicknames – that probably few Italians would know all of them.

Besides its homely, warming stews, Italy has created many sophisticated meat dishes and the most varied collection of sausages and preserved meats of any country. Almost every region has its own coastline, and so its own favoured types of fish and its special fish dishes. Native cheeses also come in all shapes, textures and flavours. Desserts are also distinctive, and vary from almost incredible richness to the deliciously refreshing.

For most Italians eating is an important occupation of immense pleasure and not to be rushed or hurried over, and they still cook with great attention to detail. Changes are of course taking place in the Italian kitchen; but slowly. The majority of Italians are not as ready as the rest of the Western world to take to convenience foods, and the use of the freezer, too, is as yet limited. Although many younger women work, they still regard cooking as an important activity.

Eating in Italy today

A typical Italian meal is still very much as it was in the eighteenth century. The main meal is taken at lunchtime, in a very leisurely fashion and accompanied by a suitable local wine. A selection of antipasti is always served, even if there is only a choice of olives, anchovies, sliced meat or raw vegetables. This is followed by either *pasta asciutta* – a cooked pasta dish with a sauce, or *pasta in brodo,* a light soup with pasta gently cooked in it. The main dish of meat or fish is rarely accompanied by vegetables: instead, salad or vegetables are served afterwards. Cheese and fruit provide the usual finish to the meal, but on special occasions a dessert is served.

The evening meal, served fairly late, is largely similar and usually consists of antipasti, followed by *pasta asciutta* or a meat or fish dish. Salad or a vegetable dish may be served, then fruit and cheese. The pattern of eating varies little from the north to the south of Italy but rather from big cities to the heart of the countryside. In cities the influence of modern patterns of working means that more people eat out at lunchtime instead of going home.

Eating out in Italy can be confusing for the visitor unless he or she knows what to look for. There is an abundance of expensive restaurants in all the big cities; but these are never the ideal places to find a regional cuisine. You will find that the locals go to a *trattoria,* a tavern, where the food is homely and the service good but simple. Or perhaps they might go to an *osteria,* a hostelry or inn, where the atmosphere is yet more informal – almost like being in someone's kitchen – where you can watch your meal being cooked for you. Only in these establishments will you find the best of the local cuisine and the real feeling of the region.

▲ This Roman relief of the second or third century BC shows a market stall with umbrella, much as today.

▼ Making pasta in a large household kitchen of the sixteenth century.

Italian regional food

The character and variety of Italian cooking is determined by two important factors. Firstly there is an inherent economic difference between the cooking of the north and of the south. Whereas the north is fertile, industrialized and heavily populated, and consequently much more affluent, the south has not such good-quality land, and is hotter and often parched. For these reasons it has always been poor and far more thinly populated. The cooking of the north frequently uses quantities of butter; but, as a general rule, the south cooks with olive oil, which it produces in abundance. Some southern cooking also uses olive oil and butter mixed. In the north, where rice is grown in quantity, rice and polenta are staple foods. Pasta, in the north, traditionally includes the flat ribbon type made with eggs, whereas the south prefers macaroni, made without eggs. The cooking of the north is often enriched by the addition of milk or cream. Dishes from the south of Italy, meanwhile, are flavoured with garlic and tomatoes more frequently than their northern counterparts.

A second regional influence is the fact that until the last century, Italy was divided into different states, each with its own culinary differences. The country's subsequent unification has had little effect on such divergencies, for, local feeling apart, most regional dishes were based upon the area's own produce, which remains not much changed. However, it is often difficult, as a visitor, to discover the best of the local cuisine. You may need to ask before any specialities are identified for you.

One of the most confusing differences to be found throughout the regions of Italy is the many names used for just one dish; for example for one type of pasta. For instance *tagliatelle* (see pp. 88-9) is known as *fettuccine* in Rome and some surrounding districts, but in other regions is called *tagliarini*. North of Venice, veal is called *vitello,* but in the south it is known as *vitella*. *Saltimbocca* is the name commonly given to a particular dish made from small slices of veal rolled or cooked flat with slices of ham or a stuffing; but in some parts of the country it is also called *bocconcini, scappati* or *involtini*. Fish, too, can each have many names: mussels, for instance, are *cozze* in the south, whereas in the north they are known as *peoci*.

The map on the opposite page gives a very simplified picture of the agricultural and culinary specialities of each region. It also sets out to show in brief the great differences between the north and the south of Italy.

Piedmont

The Piedmont region has both lush, flat valleys and harsh mountainous terrain that between them provide Italy with many of its best-known exports. These include the white truffle, which is especially prized. This rather unfamiliar species of underground fungus has a stronger flavour than the black truffle and is at its best during the winter. It is sought out by truffle-gatherers with trained dogs who detect it by scent; and usually it is dug up at night to prevent its discovery by less experienced people whose foraging might disturb the site. As a result the white truffle fetches a very high price. It has a very slight flavour of garlic and is usually served raw, thinly sliced.

Fontina
Gorgonzola
Bel Paese
Veneto
Piedmont
Lombardy
Valpolicella
Turin
Milan
Soave
orchard fruit
Campari
Borolo
Vermouth
Verona
Venice
truffles
Emilia
Romagna
Parma
prawns
Liguria
basil
Genoa
Parmesan
Bologna
mussels
Ravenna
sardines
Tuscany
squid
Florence
eel
chickens
Siena
Marche
Chianti
Umbria
Orvieto
Verdicchio
black
truffles
broccoli
figs
Lazio
Abruzzi
Pescara
Rome
Mozzarella
Frascati
Molise
Sambuca
artichokes
Campobasso
squid
tomatoes
clams
Campania
octopus
Apulia
Naples
broccoli
Salerno
fruit
Basilicata
crabs
Taranto
mussels
peppers
figs
Calabria
aubergines
Reggio
Sardinia
game
saffron
Cagliari
lobsters
Palermo
Marsala
Sicily
tomatoes
crystallized
fruits
swordfish
wheat
rice
maize
olives
citrus fruits
grapes
wines
cheese
cattle
pigs
red mullet
anchovies
tuna

The Po valley, running through Piedmont, Lombardy and Veneto, is Italy's main rice-producing area. Rice is an important product for Italy as it is different from the rice of other countries. One incidental consequence of rice cultivation in the area is that its lowland areas are rich in freshwater fish such as trout and carp. Other 'natural' sources of food include a good selection of game. Local culinary inventions include the long, thin, crisp breadsticks called *grissini,* which originated in Turin, the regional capital, and which were traditionally a great favourite of Napoleon. Some of Italy's better-known cheeses also come from Piedmont, including Robiole, Tomma Veja and, in particular, Fontina. Much Piedmontese cooking is centred round cheese. *Fonduta,* for instance, is the Italian version of a fondue but made with truffles and without alcohol, and served with polenta. *Gnocchi,* tiny dumplings, are widely eaten in Piedmont, often served with Fontina. One of the best Piedmontese dishes is *bagna cauda* – a hot anchovy-and-garlic dip served with crisp, raw vegetables.

Piedmont is also credited with producing a number of Italy's better-known drinks. Barolo is thought by many to be the finest Italian red wine and, a close second, Barbaresco, a lighter red wine. These come from the Langhe valley, not far from Asti, the home of many sparkling white wines. This region also produces a much harsher drink: Grappa, a fiery brandy, in many varieties, distilled from grape skins and pips after the wine has been tapped. Vermouth is, of course, well known throughout the world. Often thought to be of French origin, it is in fact made in both countries and has been produced in Turin to a secret recipe for over two hundred years. It is now drunk more in other countries than in Italy.

Lombardy

Milan, in the centre of Lombardy, produces the best of many generations of cooking. Although the city is now very much a business centre and has to cater for business and working lunches, both its old centre and the suburbs have many *trattoria* serving the food of the region.

Butter is important to Milanese cooking. So too is saffron, whose popularity stems from the fourteenth-century tradition of taking food to the table coloured gold wherever possible. Saffron was also thought to have medicinal properties. Many local risottos are flavoured and coloured gold, as in *osso buco,* a Milanese speciality. The expression 'alla Milanese' often refers to the use of rice, the local produce, but can also refer to the colour of

◄ Growing rice in the Po valley, in fields swamped for the purpose. Cultivating this cereal is a big industry in Piedmont and Lombardy.

▲ Fishing boats docking at the Ligurian port of Viareggio.

a particular dish. Veal cutlets, for instance, coated in egg and crumbs and fried in butter are called *costoletta alla Milanese*.

Lombardy's produce boasts the widely known Gorgonzola cheese; few people realize however that the yellow creamy cheese Bel Paese comes from this area too, as does Mascarpone, a delicate creamy cheese often served with sugar or fruit. Among puddings, *panettone* is traditional, served in this region at Christmas, and *torrone,* a rich almond-flavoured sweet, was also created here.

The wines of Lombardy are not much exported. There are some very good ones to be found locally, however, and the region does produce the widely known aperitif, Campari.

Liguria

This is predominantly a coastal region with its capital and main port, Genoa, sited in the middle. With one or two exceptions, fish dishes predominate over meat throughout the region. They include several good fish soups or stews, of which *burrida* is perhaps best known. The Genoese version of *fritto misto di mare* – a deep-fried mixture of seafoods – is another favourite.

The second, or perhaps equally important, feature of Ligurian cooking is the predominance of herbs and green vegetables. Behind the long Ligurian coastline is a rich and hilly area that provides a variety of herbs including the best basil in Italy. Basil is essential to much Genoese cooking, notably as the basis of *pesto* sauce, a sharp pungent mixture of cheeses, garlic and olive oil. This sauce is served over simple pasta dishes; with ravioli; on gnocchi; and, locally, as a sharp-flavoured topping to minestrone, which the Genoese claim to have invented also. Basil should not be chopped like most herbs, but torn into shreds. Other herbs common to this region include sage, which helps to give some meats a slightly gamey flavour. Rosemary and marjoram are also frequently used.

The Ligurian climate encourages good crops of olives, and olive oil is much used here. The region's cooking also features many delicious thick soups, and above all a local creation, ravioli. Although this was originally thought to be a clever way of using up left-over ingredients wrapped in tiny parcels of pasta, ravioli has since become a complicated and often delicate mixture of rich ingredients.

Among desserts, Ligurian cooking produces some very good sweet dishes, for instance pastries and candied fruits, and its own version of a sweet Christmas bread, known as *pandolce genovese*.

Veneto

For centuries Veneto was a centre of affluence and wealth and the culinary heart of Italy. But now, even though its cooking still keeps some quality of elegance, much has been lost to the eating demands made by the modern industry of tourism. Traditional characteristics do survive, however, including Austrian influences from the Hapsburg era which can be found in some of the names and flavour combinations of local dishes.

Fish plays a big part in the cuisine of Veneto: in particular shellfish, eels, sardines and trout, the latter from mountain lakes. The most popular ways of cooking fish here are to deep fry, charcoal or open roast. Alongside such fresh fish, *baccalá,* salted and dried cod, is also traditional to the region. After long soaking this can be cooked in many enterprising ways.

Rice is also frequently served, usually cooked with other ingredients rather than on its own. *Risi e bisi,* made with fresh young peas in their pods, is a classic Venetian dish, as are rice with scampi and rice with grapes. But perhaps more important than rice is polenta, a food made from the local maize, which is much whiter and has a finer texture than in other areas. It is served with meat and fish dishes, in particular *baccalá,* or can be served with a sauce alone.

An important salad ingredient in this part of Italy is *radicchio,* a lettuce-like plant which varies in colour from pale to deep red, depending on where it comes from, with white stalks and veins. It has a slightly stronger, more bitter flavour than lettuce.

Although there are many good wines around Venice few travel well. Those best known outside Italy are Bardolino, Valpolicella and Soave.

Emilia-Romagna

The city of Bologna is one of the culinary centres of Italy. It is surrounded by some of the most fertile land in the country, producing a variety of good raw ingredients. It is these, and the generous use of butter, cream or milk, cheese and spiced or seasoned meats, that give Bolognese cooking the reputation of being very rich.

Products of the region are well known in many other countries. Parmesan for instance, is Italy's most widely used cheese. Mortadella is thought to have been the first spiced meat – though a more famous one is *prosciutto di Parma* – a local mountain-dried ham that the rest of the world regards as a luxury.

Bologna is famed for creating such pasta dishes as tagliatelle, lasagne and tortellini (the latter is sometimes found elsewhere in the region under other names: *annelini* in Piacenza, *cappelletti* in Reggio, and *ravioli* in Modena). To accompany these pastas Bologna also created the *ragu* – in many parts of the world better known as Bolognese sauce. The true *ragu* is a very rich meat sauce with little or no tomato, unlike the version one might find in many restaurants.

It is not hard to understand why Bologna has a reputation for a heavy rich cuisine. But it is unfair not to describe it in any other way. Many of its best-known dishes combine a delicious range of local foods without any excess; for instance lasagne, with its rich *ragu* offset by a light creamy white sauce; or *petti di pollo alla Bolognese* – a carefully contrived combination of chicken, Parma ham and cheese.

Tuscany

In contrast to Bologna, Tuscany is regarded as having a more simple approach to cooking. There are far less sauces, and the flavour of the basic ingredients can be easily appreciated. The heart of Tuscan cooking comes from Florence – though not every dish called 'alla fiorentina' has to have spinach in, as we so often think.

▲ The elegant Rialto bridge in Venice overlooks a busy fish market.

▼ The lush green Tuscan vineyards produce large quantities of Chianti.

▲ An unusual view of St Peter's in Rome seen across an ice cream van selling *gelati* and *granite*.

Tuscan beef is the best in Italy, the animals being killed while still young. *Bistecca alla fiorentina* is a delicious combination of beef seasoned with olive oil, salt and pepper. The region also has a great deal of game.

Tuscan olive oil is exceptionally good and used in most local cooking. Beans, of the haricot or sometimes butter bean type, are very popular. Famous dishes like *zuppa di fagioli* come from this area, as does the delicious bean and tuna antipasto *fagioli con tonno*. Beans are also much used in meat cooking.

Best known of all Tuscan produce is Chianti, a wine appreciated all over the world. Strictly speaking it is only made in one small part of Tuscany, where it is known as 'Chianti classico'; but there are many other good versions.

Rome and Lazio

It is not surprising that Rome, in the middle of Italy, should, with its surrounding region, Lazio, have acquired the best of all things gastronomic. It combines the richer food of the north with the simple dishes of the south to produce a robust and hearty cuisine.

One of the best-known meat products of the region is *porchetta*, suckling pig stuffed with cheese, herbs and pork fat and roasted whole. The dish requires lengthy preparation and cooking and is rarely made at home these days. *Saltimbocca,* a simple yet richly flavoured combination of small pieces of veal topped with ham and fresh sage and cooked in butter and wine, is typical of Roman cuisine. So too, even though probably they originated elsewhere, are *canelloni* and *gnocchi*.

The cooking of this area has the advantage of using many good vegetables, including artichokes, broccoli, fennel and tomatoes, and also many herbs such as sage or wild mint. The most important cheese produced near Rome is Pecorino. It is very sharp and firm and improves with keeping. Frascati is one of the most popular wines native to this region. There are many other good white wines here but they are mainly only available locally. The popular ending to a meal in Rome is Sambucca, an anise-flavoured liqueur which was at one time fashionably drunk with a coffee bean flamed on top.

Umbria

North of Lazio lies Umbria, whose capital, Perugia, is the sweet-making centre of Italy. Its reputation as the source of some of the best sweets in the world reaches far and wide.

Umbria's meat products include exceptionally good pork, especially near Norcia – so much so that to many people the name has become synonymous with good butchers. Vegetables in this region are also excellent, particularly tomatoes, onions and mushrooms. The mushrooms vary in type and name: flap mushrooms, honey mushrooms and orange-milk mushrooms all have their own special characteristics. A particular speciality is black truffles, which are often exported to France. In Umbria they are served in a delicious spaghetti sauce, having been marinaded in olive oil, garlic and anchovy paste.

The only Umbrian wine especially well known outside Italy is Orvieto, which is produced on the borders of Umbria and Lazio. This was formerly produced only as a sweet wine; but there is now also a dry version.

The Marches

To the east of Umbria, the Marches take in an extensive section of the Adriatic coast. Their gastronomic speciality is fish – not surprisingly, as Ancona, Italy's principal fishing port, is at the centre of the area.

► Pasta shops throughout Italy sell as many varieties and shapes as they can find room for.

▲ Southern Italians love sweet foods, like these sugared almonds, which are used to create exotic decorations.

Fish from the Marches also goes to Umbria, which lacks a coastline of its own and takes its local fresh fish from inland lakes. The fish soups and stews of the Marches are excellent and very varied and use some interesting combinations of flavours. Other outstanding food products from the Marches mainly include vegetables, and Verdicchio, a yellowish-green wine which is increasingly popular outside Italy.

Abruzzi and Molise

Travelling south towards Naples, the difference in terrain from north to south, and consequently the wealth and eating habits of the people, becomes very apparent. The land is more mountainous in the south, and poorer in quality. There is a small quantity of lamb eaten in this area and some local ham is cured. Chicken is popular, as the birds are not too expensive to keep.

Along the coast, fish is plentiful, and used in many different dishes, often with the particular characteristics imparted by the Abruzzi wine vinegars. Many dishes are strongly flavoured with peppers, sometimes to the extent of being quite fiery.

One important speciality of Abruzzi that is occasionally exported is saffron, a mild flavouring and source of colouring that cannot be replaced by anything else. The little yellow strands of saffron that, when soaked in water, give off its especial colour and flavour are the stamens of a crocus flower. Very few are available from each flower head and they don't go very far in cooking, so saffron is a very expensive product.

Naples and Campania

Naples is the industrial and culinary centre of the south of Italy and has produced some of the most renowned Italian dishes. In Campania as a whole, though the region is not as poor as many surrounding areas, a sense of economy does prevail. Neapolitan cooking has a certain flourish and flamboyance to it, expressing a determination to live happily and eat well at all times. It is often brightly coloured and piquantly flavoured, for example in the form of pizzas, or macaroni and spaghetti dishes in pizzaiola sauce. The local dishes also use small quantities of many ingredients, are made quickly and can be eaten simply.

Many types of cereal and vegetables grow well in this region, especially the tomato, which is virtually a staple of Neapolitan cooking. Among cheeses, Mozzarella is made here, and served in a rather unusual way – in *carrozza* ('a carriage') – in a fried-bread sandwich.

▲ A view of Naples — where the pizza was invented and is still the most popular local dish.

► Most Italian types of cheese, like the Pecorino in this picture, are still made by hand, often on a very small scale.

Off the coast of Campania shellfish, frequently used in pasta sauces, have for long been the most prolific of several forms of seafood. It was in the area of Naples that it was first discovered how to farm oysters.

It was also the Neapolitans who discovered how to dry and keep pasta. In many parts of the country it is customary to buy newly made pasta while it is still moist; in the south of Italy, though, rather more dry pasta is bought than in the north. Other Neapolitan dishes include a range of ices, or *gelati,* and *granite,* or water ices, first introduced to this part of Italy from the East.

Apulia

This region relies heavily for its food on the resources of its long coastline. Swordfish, eels, sardines, anchovies, and octopus in particular, are used in many of its dishes. Oysters, too, from the Gulf of Taranto, are eaten here.

Cabbage, turnip, garlic, peppers, aubergines, olives and almonds provide some of the best produce in the area. Very little meat is available, however, and the Apulians use quantities of vegetable to make several forms of meat sauce go further.

Apulia, like many other regions, has its own pasta speciality, known as *laganelle,* a small stuffed lasagne similar to cannelloni. It also produces good wines, although few are exported either abroad or to other parts of Italy.

Calabria

In Italy, the farther south, the drier the climate and the more difficult the land becomes to cultivate. Aubergines are one of the few vegetables that do grow well here and are used in a large number of dishes. In one popular recipe in particular,

▲ Around the coast of Sicily, tuna fishing takes the form of a spectacular annual battle with these huge creatures.

aubergines are served having been marinaded in a mixture of vinegar, basil and garlic. Although much pork and offal is eaten, a great deal of meat is made into sausages of many varieties. Soups, thickened with pasta, often form the main part of the meal and bread is very important to the diet.

Many cheeses are made here, but only for local consumption. To add excitement to the rather austere traditional diet there is a wide range of sticky sweet puddings, heavy cakes, biscuits and glamorous desserts.

Sicily

This beautiful island depends largely for its diet on several species of fish. Above all it is the heart of the Italian tuna fish industry.

It is here every spring that a big annual catch is penned and killed, in an enclosure that turns into a turmoil of huge floundering fish as the tuna are gradually cornered and caught. Sicily is dependent on the netting, canning and exporting of tuna for much of its livelihood. The fresh tuna eaten on the island itself is, however, very different to the product most people buy in tins and is essential to many delicious Italian recipes. *Vitello tonnato,* for instance, combining cold braised veal with a creamy tuna mayonnaise, has become popular in restaurants around the world.

Swordfish, hunted in much the same way as tuna, is also important to Sicily, as are sardines, which are locally served freshly fried on street stalls. Though the island is rich in fish, its sources of meat are limited mainly to rabbit, pork or cured meats.

Most Sicilian cooking is done with olive oil; tomatoes, too, are widely used. The best-known local cheese is Caciocavallo. Fruits, vegetables and cereals grow in abundance, and over the years a number of them have lent themselves to the creation of a repertoire of delicious confectionery and desserts, such as *cassata siciliana* and *zabaione*. The latter, a light, fluffy egg dessert, relies for much of its flavour on another local product, Marsala, a dessert wine first made by an Englishman, and just one of a range of good Sicilian wines.

Sardinia

In contrast to Sicily, Sardinia is largely barren, and little grows easily here. Fruit, wine and vegetable production is generally confined to small quantities in limited areas. There is a substantial fishing industry, but inland life in the mountainous areas is primitive by comparison. Hunting is still an important means of providing the family with meat or game, and wild boar and sometimes even bear are killed for food. Kid, suckling pig and many small birds are also frequently eaten.

▲ The wild boars of Sardinia are still hunted as a prized source of food.

The Sardinians are still great practitioners of spit or open roasting, having practised it for many generations out of necessity. Their meat cooking includes some excellent flavour combinations: roast pork with myrtle, for instance.

Bread is important to the local diet, and is freshly made every day. The Sardinians also produce a cheese called Pecorino.

► Overleaf, top left to right: *scampi alla griglia; bagna cauda; sardine fritte; prosciutto con melone; insalata di mozzarella; fagioli toscanelli con tonno;* front row fresh salad vegetables and fruit; *insalata di finocchi; funghi porchini al tegame.*

Antipasti

The antipasti, or starters, can be immensely varied, including cold meat, fish or vegetable dishes, and hot mixtures or crisp toasts.

Mozzarella in carrozza (fried cheese sandwiches)

South of Rome this tasty dish is as popular as bacon and eggs in England or *raclettes* in Switzerland.

Serves 3-4

oil for frying
1 small sliced white loaf
225 g (8 oz) fresh Mozzarella
2 eggs
a little milk

In a large pan heat the oil until a tiny piece of bread then placed in it turns golden in 45 seconds. Meanwhile cut the bread into 4-cm rounds with a pastry cutter. Cut the cheese into slightly smaller rounds, about $\frac{1}{2}$cm thick. Put each sandwich together. Beat the eggs with a couple of tablespoons of milk. Dip the sandwiches in this mixture briefly. Then pop them into the hot fat for 1-2 minutes, until crisp and golden. Drain on kitchen paper before serving.

Insalata di mozzarella (Mozzarella and tomato salad)

Serves 3-4

4 large tomatoes, sliced
225 g (8 oz) fresh Mozzarella
2-3 sprigs fresh sage
salt
olive oil
fresh ground black pepper

Slice the tomatoes onto a large, flat serving plate. Then thickly slice the cheese and arrange neatly in the centre of the plate. Chop half the sage, add to the dish, and sprinkle over with salt. Pour oil generously over the cheese and tomatoes and then sprinkle with black pepper. Garnish with the remaining sage leaves. Chill for 1 hour before serving.

Bagna cauda (hot anchovy and garlic dip)

Literally translated, this means 'a hot bath'. In this case it is a hot sauce served with raw, crisp vegetables. Some versions in Italy contain fresh white truffles but it can be made quite successfully without them. Like many dishes from the Piedmont region it calls for a large proportion of cream to give it its distinctive flavour.

Serves 4-6

100 g (4 oz) butter
1 clove garlic, chopped
8 anchovy fillets (drain well if you use canned anchovy)
250 ml ($\frac{1}{2}$ pint) double cream

Melt the butter and gently cook the garlic until soft but not browned. Add the anchovy fillets and beat in until smooth. Then add the cream, beat thoroughly and then bring to the boil. Cook for 2-3 minutes until thickened. Serve hot at the table in a fondue pan if possible, with a selection of crisp raw vegetables like cucumber, carrot, green pepper or celery, cut into thin strips.

Funghi porcini al tegame (mushrooms with garlic and mint)

This dish originated in Rome where the distinctive flavour of the cooking is said to come from the soil – sun-scorched and volcanic.

Serves 6

900 g (2 lb) mushrooms, preferably the large flat field ones
6 tablespoons oil
2-3 anchovy fillets, chopped
2 cloves garlic, crushed
6 large tomatoes, peeled and finely chopped
2-3 sprigs of fresh mint, chopped, or 1 heaped teaspoonful, dried
salt and black pepper

Wash the mushrooms and slice them evenly. Heat the oil with the anchovies and garlic and mix until the anchovies dissolve almost to a paste. Add the mushrooms, tomatoes and mint. Add the seasonings, and cover. Allow to simmer gently for about 15 minutes, stirring occasionally. Serve with croutons of hot fried bread.

Scampi alla griglia (prawns in garlic butter)

Serves 4-6

1 kg (2 lb) fresh prawns in their shells or 500 g (1 lb) shelled prawns or scampi
100 g (4 oz) butter
4 tablespoons olive oil
1 tablespoon lemon juice
1 tiny onion or shallot, very finely chopped
3 cloves garlic, crushed
$\frac{1}{2}$ teaspoon salt
freshly ground black pepper
3 tablespoons parsley, chopped
lemon pieces to garnish

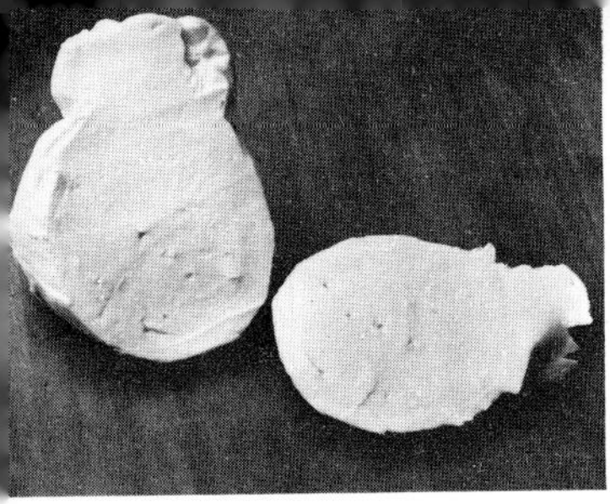

▲ Always try to use Mozzarella fresh – it will be moister and have a more subtle flavour.

Shell the prawns, leaving a small piece on the tail (to help eat with the fingers if you wish). With a small sharp knife, slit down the back of the prawn and remove the black vein. Wash and dry the prawns. Meanwhile melt the butter and oil in a large pan and add the lemon juice, shallot and garlic. Toss the prawns in this, then arrange on the grill tray and place under a hot grill for about 8 minutes, basting with the butter mixture and turning once. Add the seasoning and the parsley to the butter, and pour this sauce on the hot cooked prawns. Serve with lemon wedges.

Fagioli toscanelli con tonno (bean and tuna fish salad)

Serves 4

a 450-g (15½-oz) can cannellini or haricot beans or 225 g (8 oz) dried haricot or butter beans, cooked
3 tablespoons olive oil
2 tablespoons lemon juice
salt
freshly ground black pepper
1 small onion, finely chopped
2 tablespoons parsley, chopped
a 225-g (7-oz) can tuna fish

If using canned beans drain and then rinse them in cold water. For dried beans, soak for 2 hours, then simmer gently in 1½ litres (3 pints) of water until just tender. Drain. Mix together the oil, lemon juice and seasoning. Add the beans, onion and parsley and chill well. Flake the fish into chunks and just before serving arrange on top of the beans.

Crostini di fegatini di pollo (chicken livers on toast)

Serves 6

225 g (8 oz) chicken livers
1 tablespoon olive oil
2 tablespoons butter or lard
1 small onion, sliced
1 sprig fresh sage, or 1 teaspoon dried sage, chopped
salt and pepper
6 slices of bread
lemon juice
1 tablespoon grated Parmesan

Wash the livers and chop finely. Heat the oil and butter or lard and gently fry the onion until golden. Add the livers and sage, season, and then simmer for 10 minutes. Meanwhile toast the bread. Add a few drops of lemon juice to the livers with the cheese, remove the sage leaves and spoon the mixture onto the toast. Heat through in the oven if necessary.

Sardine fritte (fresh sardines fried)

3 small sardines, or 1 larger one, per person
salt and freshly ground black pepper
juice of 1 large lemon
a little butter

If the sardines are very small just clean them out and leave them whole. The large ones can be slit right down the middle on the underside and opened out. Sprinkle the sardines with salt, pepper and lots of lemon juice and grill or bake in the oven or over a barbecue if you have one. Otherwise fry quickly in butter and lemon juice. Brush the grilled sardines with a little melted butter before serving.

Insalata di finocchi (fennel salad)

Serves 4

½ cucumber, chopped
1 large head of fennel
3-4 radishes, sliced
salt and pepper
pinch of dried mint or 1 teaspoon fresh mint, chopped
olive oil
lemon juice
1 orange, peeled and cut into segments

Place the cucumber in a large bowl. Trim the ends off the fennel then cut it into thin slices. Add to the cucumber with the radishes and seasoning. Mix the mint, oil and lemon juice to taste and pour over the vegetables, adding the orange segments at the last minute.

Pasta

This is simple food, simply cooked and eaten. But it can provide one of the world's most delicious dishes, and its range of shapes, textures and flavours is almost endless.

Tagliatelle all'uovo (homemade egg noodles)

Makes nearly 450 g (1 lb)

175 g (6 oz) plain flour
1 egg
2-3 tablespoons olive oil
½ teaspoon salt
a little water

Put the flour into a large mixing bowl or onto a clean working surface. Sprinkle the salt over and make a well in the middle of the flour. Lightly beat the egg and oil together and pour into the centre of the flour. Start mixing together using either a fork or your hands.

Gradually add a few spoonfuls of cold water to help bring together all the

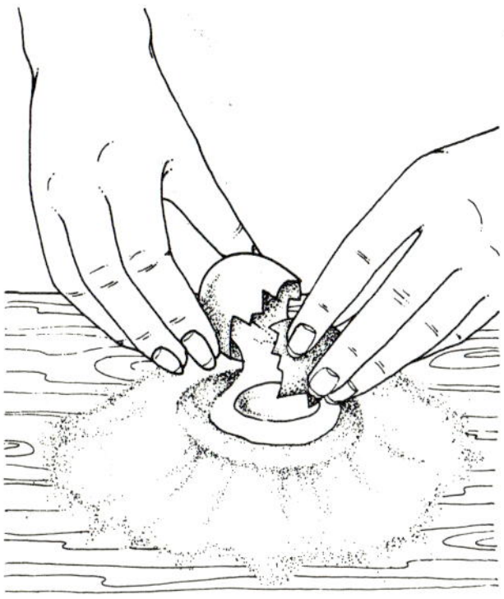

loose flour and then knead for about 10 minutes on a

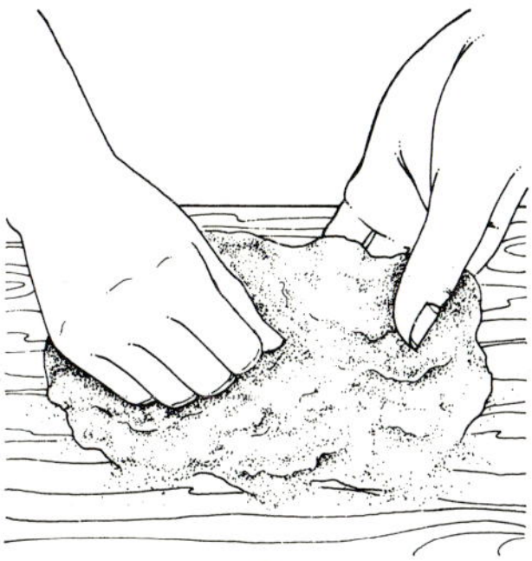

floured surface until the dough becomes smooth and shiny.

Wrap the dough in greaseproof paper and leave for about 10 minutes. Divide it into two to make it easier to handle. Then roll out the dough to a long thin oblong.

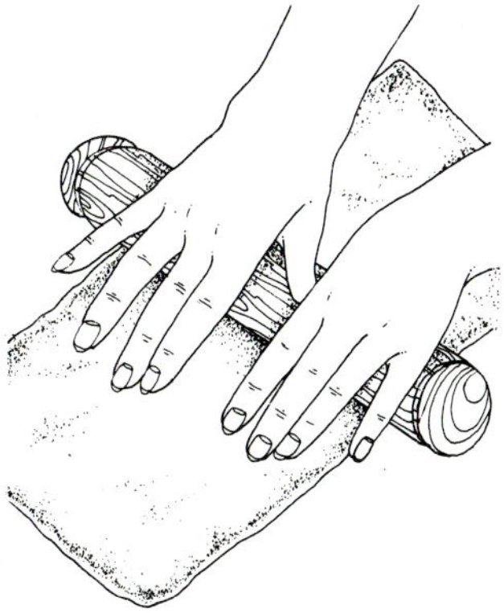

Keep rolling until the dough is paper thin and you can see through it. Dust the surface with extra flour if necessary. Brush off any excess flour but make sure the top of the dough has a thin, even

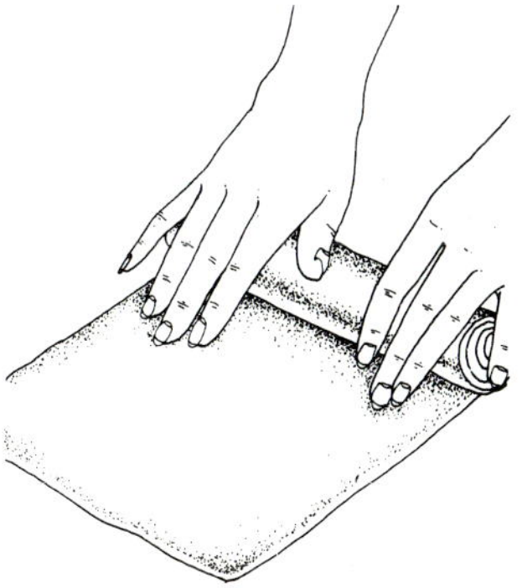

coating. Leave for 10 minutes, covered.

Gently roll the dough from one narrow end into a long sausage shape.

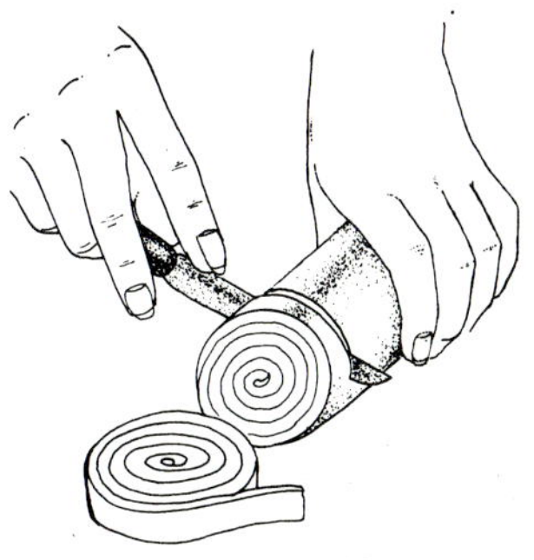

With a sharp knife cut this into ½-cm-even strips. Avoid pressing too hard or the layers of dough will stick together. Carefully unroll each strip of dough and lay

out flat or hang for a few minutes. Then roll out and repeat the process with the remaining dough. To store these noodles, wrap them in a polythene bag and keep in a refrigerator for a day or two.

To cook immediately, bring a pan of salted water to the boil. Even for a small amount of pasta you should use at least 3 litres (6 pints) of water. When the water is really boiling add the pasta all at once and bring back to the boil. Stir once or twice with a wooden spoon to keep each piece separate. Allow to boil for about 6 minutes, until just tender. This condition is known as *al dente*, which, literally, means 'to the tooth' – when you bite it it still feels firm in the centre. Drain the pasta, and return to the pan or place in a serving dish with a knob of butter or a little oil. Serve immediately with freshly grated Parmesan cheese, or toss in sauce according to the recipe used.

Cooking times for bought pasta

These vary according to the pasta's size and shape. A good rule is to test it 3-4 minutes before the time stated on the packet.

Pasta alla caprese (pasta with tomatoes and tuna)

Serves 4

350 g (12 oz) tomatoes
4 tablespoons olive oil
salt and freshly ground black pepper
4-5 anchovy fillets, drained
100 g (4 oz) canned tuna
4-6 stoned black olives, finely chopped
450 g (1 lb) farfalle (pasta 'bows': see p. 88)
75-100 g (3-4 oz) Mozzarella cheese, diced

Peel and chop the tomatoes and gently fry in the hot oil with little salt for about 15 minutes, stirring frequently. Pound the drained anchovy and tuna to a paste. Add the olives and heat through gently in a separate pan. Meanwhile cook the pasta bows as directed on p. 25 and drain when still just firm. Toss immediately in the two hot sauces with the Mozzarella and the pepper.

▲ Home-made pasta can be flavoured and enriched in several different ways. Some of the most common ingredients are spinach, paprika, mustard, peppers or eggs.

Tagliatelle all'amatriciana (noodles Amatrice style)

This famous dish takes its name from the town of Amatrice in the Sabine Hills, just outside Rome.

Serves 4

450 g (1 lb) tagliatelle
2 tablespoons oil
1 onion, thinly sliced
100 g (4 oz) lean bacon, diced
small glass dry white wine
350 g (12 oz) tomatoes
salt and pepper
50 g (2 oz) grated Parmesan
1 teaspoon fresh rosemary, chopped

Cook the tagliatelle as directed on p. 25. Meanwhile heat the oil and fry the onion and bacon for a few minutes. Add the wine and cook until it has reduced slightly. Add the tomatoes, peeled and chopped, and the seasoning and simmer for about 15 minutes, stirring occasionally. When the pasta is cooked, drain and toss immediately in the hot sauce. Serve sprinkled with the cheese and the rosemary.

Rigatoni alla carbonara (ribbed pasta with bacon and egg sauce)

This dish originated in Rome in the days when most foods were cooked over charcoal burners – the meaning of 'carbonara'.

Serves 4

450 g (1 lb) rigatoni (see p. 88)
6 rashers streaky bacon, chopped
2 eggs

1 tablespoon cream (optional)
100 g (4 oz) grated Parmesan
salt

Cook the rigatoni as on p. 25 until still only just firm. Meanwhile fry the chopped bacon gently until the fat runs out and the bacon becomes crisp. Beat together the eggs, cream and half of the cheese. When the pasta is cooked, drain and return to the pan. Add the bacon and fat and then stir in the eggs. Heat gently, stirring until the eggs scramble very softly to make a creamy sauce. Season if necessary and serve with extra cheese.

Spaghetti bolognese (spaghetti in meat sauce)

This rich ragu (meat sauce) is one of the classics of Bolognese cooking. It is used for many pork or veal dishes, for filling ravioli or in lasagne and cannelloni. In Bologna it traditionally has 125-250 ml ($\frac{1}{4}$-$\frac{1}{2}$ pint) of cream or milk added during cooking to the quantities given here.

Serves 4-6

225 g (8 oz) lean minced beef
75 g (3 oz) bacon or uncooked ham, chopped
50 g (2 oz) butter
2 tablespoons olive oil
100 g (4 oz) chicken livers
1 carrot, diced
1 onion, chopped
1 small stick celery, chopped
3 teaspoons tomato purée
1 glass white wine
2 glasses stock
salt and pepper
$\frac{1}{2}$ teaspoon ground nutmeg
450 g (1 lb) spaghetti
grated Parmesan

Fry the beef and chopped ham in butter and oil for 3-4 minutes. Then add the minced or chopped chicken livers and remaining ingredients, except for the spaghetti and cheese. Simmer gently for about 40 minutes, stirring occasionally. Meanwhile cook the spaghetti as directed on p. 25 and when still just firm, drain, and toss in the sauce. Top with the grated cheese.

Pesto alla genovese (basil, garlic and cheese sauce)

This sauce comes from Genoa where the local basil is supposed to be the best in the world. It is more like a paste than a sauce and is often used as a topping for minestrone or on gnocchi. It has a very sharp rich flavour.

Makes enough for 4 helpings of pasta

50 g (2 oz) fresh basil leaves, chopped, or substitute 50 g chopped parsley
$\frac{1}{4}$ teaspoon salt
$\frac{1}{4}$ teaspoon freshly ground black pepper
$\frac{3}{4}$ teaspoon garlic, finely chopped
5 teaspoons pine nuts or walnuts, finely chopped
125 ml ($\frac{1}{4}$ pint) olive oil
50 g (2 oz) freshly grated Parmesan

Blend all the ingredients together in a liquidizer until you have a smooth purée, or pound the dry ingredients together to a paste and then work in the oil and seasoning gradually. Serve with hot spaghetti or vermicelli, cooked as directed on p. 25 and tossed in butter and then well tossed in the sauce.

Salsa di pomodoro alla napoletana (Neapolitan tomato sauce)

Makes about 750 ml (1$\frac{1}{2}$ pints)

1 kg (2$\frac{1}{2}$ lb) ripe or canned tomatoes
3 cloves garlic, crushed
125 ml ($\frac{1}{4}$ pint) olive oil
1 tablespoon basil, chopped
1 tablespoon parsley, chopped
salt and pepper
1 teaspoon fresh oregano, chopped (optional)

Peel and chop the tomatoes. Fry the garlic in the oil until browned and then discard. Add the tomatoes, basil and parsley and seasoning and simmer gently for about 30 minutes. Add the oregano only at the last minute.

▲ Basil and thyme, two of the many herbs used in Italian cooking.

Ravioli

Makes about 50 pieces, and serves 4-5 for a main meal

1 quantity of the egg noodle dough given on p. 25
350 g (12 oz) Ricotta, or cottage cheese sieved and mixed with 3 tablespoons cream
100 g (4 oz) freshly grated Parmesan
2 teaspoons grated onion
3 egg yolks
1 teaspoon salt
½ quantity of the tomato sauce given on p. 27 or same quantity of Bolognese sauce given on p. 27.

Carefully blend together the cheeses, onion, egg yolks and salt until creamy. Put aside until required. Divide the dough in four, keeping each piece wrapped in a cloth while you roll out the others. On a floured surface, roll out one piece into an

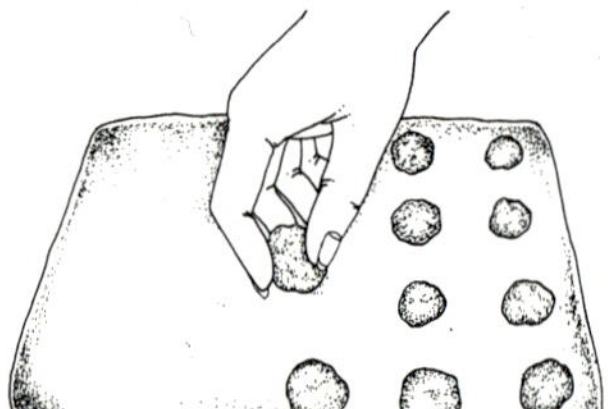

oblong. The dough should be as thin as possible. Cover with a cloth while you roll

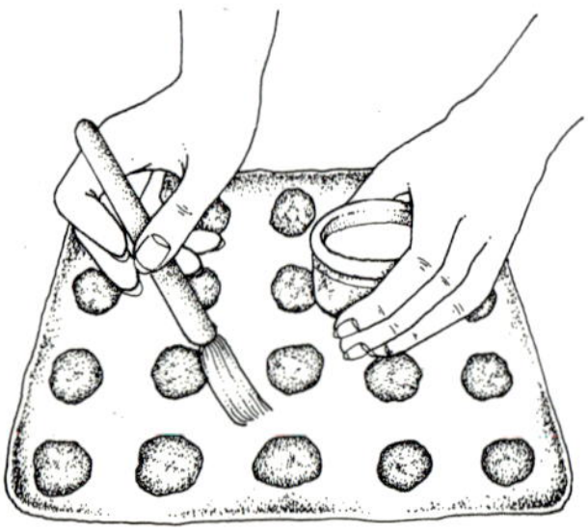

out the other pieces to the same size.

Place teaspoons of the cheese mixture at regular intervals about 2 cm apart, on two pieces of dough.

Brush horizontal and vertical lines of water between the cheese mixture to help seal the dough. Use enough water to wet it.

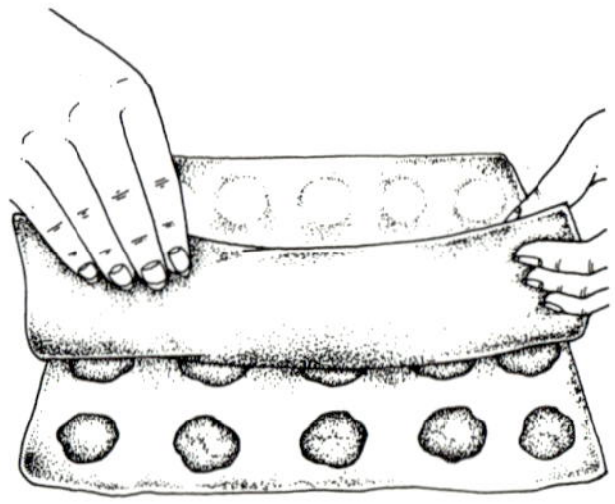

Carefully spread the other sheets of dough on top.

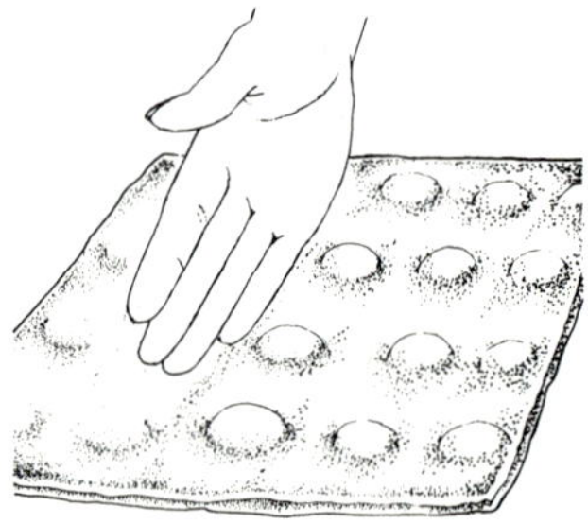

With your finger gently press around the filling along the water lines.

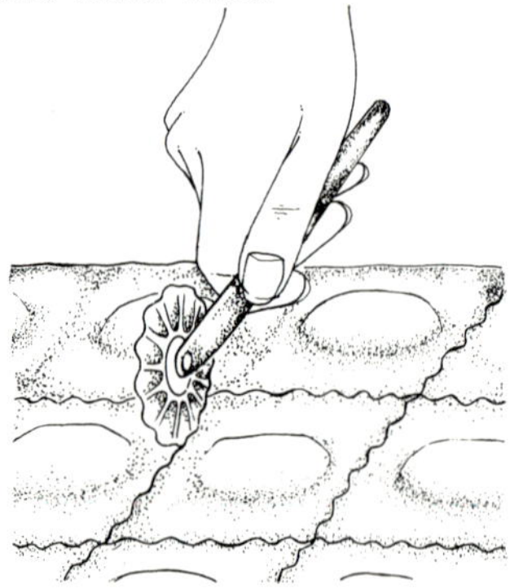

With a pastry cutter or a sharp knife (though with a knife you will not get the traditional curly edges), cut straight lines between the mounds of filling. Separate the pieces of ravioli and place on greaseproof paper until ready to cook. Cover.

To cook ravioli

Drop the ravioli into a large pan with plenty of boiling salted water. Stir with a wooden spoon to keep them from sticking and boil for about 8 minutes, until just tender. Drain, and serve immediately with melted butter and Bolognese sauce or tomato sauce.

Ravioli verdi (spinach ravioli)

Serves 4

37 g (1½ oz) butter
25 g (1 oz) chopped onion
350 g (12 oz) minced pork, veal or chicken
350 g (12 oz) fresh or a 300-g (10-oz) packet of frozen spinach
50 g (2 oz) Parmesan
pinch of nutmeg
2-3 eggs, beaten
salt and pepper
1 quantity of dough given on p. 25

Melt the butter and fry the onion and the meat gently until lightly coloured and well mixed. Transfer to a bowl. Cook and thoroughly drain the spinach, then chop finely. Add to the meat with the remaining ingredients

► Clockwise from the front: *canelloni al forno; ravioli con salsa di pomadora; lasagne verdi di carnevale.*

and mix thoroughly. Make the ravioli as explained on p. 28, and cook. Serve with melted butter and plenty of Parmesan cheese, or top with Neapolitan tomato sauce (see p. 27) and Parmesan.

Tortellini di Bologna

These are smaller than ravioli, and shaped like little hats (see p. 88). They can be served filled with any of the previous mixtures or this richer filling.

Makes about 40, to serve 4 for a main course or 8-10 in a soup.

37 g (1½ oz) butter
100 g (4 oz) pork fillet
50 g (2 oz) chicken breast
2-3 thin slices Parma ham
4-5 slices mortadella (see p. 84)
100 g (4 oz) Parmesan
2 eggs, lightly beaten
salt and pepper
grated nutmeg
1 quantity of dough as given on p. 24

Thinly slice the pork and chicken. Melt the butter, add the pork and chicken, and gently fry until golden. Mince with the ham and mortadella. Then mix with the cheese, eggs, nutmeg and seasoning. Roll out the dough in two sections and, with a 2-4-cm plain pastry cutter or a liqueur glass cut into circles. Put about a ½ teaspoon of filling on each one and brush the edges with water. Fold into semi-circles and then twist round your finger so the two ends overlap. Seal well. Cook as directed for ravioli, for about 5 minutes, and then drain. Serve with meat or tomato sauce, or simply with cream and Parmesan cheese. These 'little hats' are also very good cooked in consommé or stock and served as a nourishing accompaniment to the soup.

Lasagne verdi di carnevale (lasagne with cheese and spiced susages in tomato sauce)

Serves 6

450 g (1 lb) *lasagne verdi* sheets (see p. 88)
225 g (8 oz) Italian pork sausages or garlic sausages
250 ml (½ pint) Bolognese sauce (see p. 27)
250 ml (½ pint) tomato sauce (see p. 27)
450 g (1 lb) Ricotta cheese or good cottage cheese
75 g (3 oz) Parmesan, grated
2 eggs, beaten
salt and pepper
175 g (6 oz) Mozzarella
25 g (1 oz) butter

Cook the lasagne in plenty of boiling salted water, a few sheets at a time. Drain on a clean tea towel when just tender. Test 4-5 minutes before the end of the recommended cooking time on the packet. Fry the sausages without any extra fat, then remove the skins and slice or crumble the sausages. Heat the Bolognese and tomato sauces together. Beat the Ricotta cheese with half the Parmesan, the eggs and the seasoning. Spread this mixture on all but four or five sheets of lasagne. Place a layer in the base of a greased ovenproof dish. Cover with a little sausage, a few slices of Mozzarella, a few spoonfuls of the sauce and a generous sprinkling of Parmesan. Repeat these layers until all the ingredients are used up, finishing with the plain lasagne and a thick layer of cheese sauce. Dot with butter and bake at 190° C, 375° F/Gas 5 for about 45 minutes.

Cannelloni al forno (Rolled pasta stuffed with meat and baked with tomato and cream sauce)

Serves 4-6

450 g (1 lb) cannelloni tubes (see p. 88) or lasagne sheets
1 quantity of Bolognese sauce given on p. 27, cold
125 ml (¼ pint) tomato sauce (see p. 27)

250 ml (½ pint) Béchamel sauce:

salt and pepper
1 onion, quartered
3 bay leaves
19 g (¾ oz) butter
19 g (¾ oz) flour
250 ml (½ pint) milk, warmed
freshly grated nutmeg
2-3 tablespoons double cream
50 g (2 oz) grated Parmesan

Cook the cannelloni or lasagne as described in the previous recipe, and drain. Fill the tubes of cannelloni with the meat sauce (use a piping bag to make this easier) or spread the sheets of lasagne with sauce and roll up into tubes. To make the Béchamel sauce simmer the milk with the onion, bay leaves and seasonings for 10 minutes. Strain. Melt the butter and stir in the flour. Cook for 1 minute. Gradually whisk in the milk. Bring to the boil and cook for 1-2 minutes, whisking all the time. Season, and add the freshly grated nutmeg and cream.

Pour about a third of the two sauces into the base of a greased ovenproof dish. Arrange the filled tubes on top, covering the first layer with more sauce. Top with the rest of the sauce and a generous sprinkling of cheese. Bake at 190° C, 375° F/Gas 5 for about 35 minutes.

Lasagne con la ricotta (lasagne with mushroom and spinach sauces and ricotta topping)
Serves 6

450 g (1 lb) lasagne sheets
50 g (2 oz) butter
1 small onion, chopped
450 g (1 lb) mushrooms
1 clove garlic, crushed
salt and pepper
350 g (12 oz) fresh spinach or a 275-g (10-oz) packet frozen spinach
225 g (8 oz) minced ham
175 g (6 oz) Ricotta cheese or cottage cheese
2 tablespoons double cream
80 g (3 oz) grated Parmesan

Cook the lasagne as directed for *lasagne verdi* and drain. Melt 25 g (1 oz) of butter and fry the onion and mushrooms with the garlic and seasoning gently for about 10 minutes until soft. Cook the spinach, drain well and chop. Fry in the remaining butter with the ham. Beat the Ricotta, cream and half the Parmesan together until smooth. Arrange a layer of lasagne in the base of a greased ovenproof dish, cover with a layer of mushroom sauce, then lasagne, then spinach sauce. Repeat until all these ingredients are used up, finishing with a layer of lasagne. Top with the cheese sauce and the rest of the Parmesan. Bake at 190° C, 375° F/Gas 5 for about 45 minutes.

Pasta salads

Although rarely served cold in Italy, pasta does provide a very good basis for many substantial and unusual salads, for hot or cold weather. It gives a change in colour and texture from most salad ingredients and will blend well with numerous flavours, as we have already seen.

If you plan to serve pasta cold, cook in exactly the same way as directed on p. 25, but be sure to undercook rather than overcook. Once it is cooked, drain, but do not rinse in cold water as often recommended or you will lose all flavour and goodness. Just toss immediately in an oil and vinegar dressing, or a light creamy mayonnaise or other dressing suited to the salad you are making. When the pasta is hot it will readily absorb flavours, and the dressing will prevent the strands from sticking together. Leave to cool and then add any other ingredients, or mix before cooling, but remember the finished salad will benefit from being really cold. Allow 75-100 g (3-4 oz) of uncooked pasta per person for a main course. Here are some ideas to try:

1 Toss pasta in a garlic-flavoured dressing, and add chopped tomatoes, sliced cooked squid and chopped artichoke hearts.

2 Toss pasta in tomato-flavoured mayonnaise pepped up with a few drops of tabasco sauce. Add peeled prawns, chopped avocado and black olives.

3 Toss pasta in a little Neapolitan tomato sauce (see p. 27). Mix in chopped salame or Parma ham, and sliced Mozzarella.

Timballo di maccheroni (macaroni baked with aubergines)

This dish comes from Calabria where aubergines grow especially well and are used in much of the local cooking.

Serves 4

3 aubergines
olive oil
1 clove garlic, crushed
450 g (1 lb) tomatoes, peeled and sliced
salt and pepper
350 g (12 oz) macaroni
40 g ($1\frac{1}{2}$ oz) Pecorino or Parmesan, grated
1 sprig fresh basil, chopped, or $\frac{1}{4}$ teaspoon dried basil

Peel the aubergines, slice lengthwise and then fry in hot oil until golden. Drain on kitchen paper and keep hot. Pour off any excess fat and fry the garlic. Add the tomatoes, season, and cook for about 10 minutes. Meanwhile cook the macaroni as recommended on p. 25, until just tender, drain, and toss in the hot sauce. Place a layer in the base of a greased ovenproof dish. Cover with a layer of aubergine, then a little basil and cheese, and repeat until all the ingredients are used up, finishing with a layer of sauce and cheese. Bake at 220° C, 425° F/Gas 7 for about 15 minutes, until very hot.

Spaghetti con zucchine (spaghetti with courgette)

This is an unusual way of serving spaghetti and found in only one or two regions of Italy.

Serves 4

450 g (1 lb) small courgettes
50 g (2 oz) butter
3-4 tablespoons olive oil
salt and black pepper
225 g (8 oz) spaghetti
Parmesan, grated

Slice the unpeeled courgettes and fry in butter and oil until really tender. Cook the spaghetti as directed on p. 25, and drain and toss immediately in the courgette mixture. Sprinkle with cheese before serving.

Pasta in brodo con fegatini e piselli (pasta in chicken broth with chicken livers and peas)

Serves 4

100 g (4 oz) ready-made pasta soup shapes or 100 g (4 oz) pasta dough recipe on p. 25
75 g (3 oz) chicken livers
25 g (1 oz) butter
275 g (10 oz) peas, freshly shelled, or frozen and allowed to thaw
1 litre (2 pints) fresh chicken stock
salt and pepper
12 g ($\frac{1}{2}$ oz) Parmesan, grated

If using ready-made pasta, cook for 3-4 minutes in boiling salted water and then drain. If using homemade dough cut it into very very thin short noodles. Fry the finely chopped livers in the butter for only 1 minute. Bring the stock to the boil and add the pasta. Cook for 2 minutes. Add the peas, liver and seasoning and simmer for a further minute. Sprinkle with Parmesan cheese and serve.

Minestrone

Many regions of Italy claim to have invented the hearty vegetable soup. Their recipes all vary according to which vegetables are locally abundant and whether pasta is included, or beans. This version comes from Genoa.

Serves 4

100 g (4 oz) dried white haricot beans
salt
1 onion, sliced
2 stalks celery, diced
1 carrot, sliced
3 tablespoons olive oil
1-2 courgettes, sliced
2 small potatoes, diced
2 large tomatoes, peeled and chopped
small bunch fresh parsley or 1 tablespoon, dried
100 g (4 oz) 'elbow' macaroni
1 tablespoon pesto sauce (see p. 27)
$1\frac{1}{2}$ tablespoons Parmesan, grated

Put the beans in a large pan with $1\frac{1}{2}$ litres (3 pints) of boiling water. Soak for 1 hour. Add the salt, onion, celery, carrot and oil. Bring to the boil and simmer for 1 hour. Add the courgettes, potatoes, tomatoes and parsley. Continue cooking for another 30 minutes. Then add the macaroni and cook until just tender. Finally stir in the pesto sauce and the cheese.

► Six kinds of pizza. Clockwise from the top: Neapolitan; mussels; onion and olive; pepper and ham; sardine; mushroom.

Pizzas

Our fast-food world has readily adopted the pizza as an easy-to-eat meal and serves it up at any time. But the pizza as commonly sold is a far cry from the real thing, which is crisp, yet soft centred, and succulently topped with many fresh flavours.

Pizza

One large pizza serves 1 person as a main meal

12 g ($\frac{1}{2}$ oz) fresh yeast or 6 g ($\frac{1}{4}$ oz) dried yeast
pinch of sugar
125 ml ($\frac{1}{4}$ pint) lukewarm water
200 g (7 oz) plain flour
$\frac{1}{2}$ teaspoon salt
4-5 tablespoons olive oil
165 ml ($\frac{1}{3}$ pint) pizzaiola sauce (see below)
225 g (8 oz) Mozzarella, diced or grated
3 tablespoons Parmesan, grated

Dissolve the yeast with the sugar in 2 tablespoons of warm water. Leave for about 10 minutes in a warm place until frothy. Meanwhile sieve the flour into a warm bowl with the salt. Make a well in the centre and pour in the yeast mixture and the remaining liquid.

Mix together until it all comes clean from the sides of the bowl. Add a little water if necessary to bind.

Turn out onto a floured surface and knead well for about 5 minutes, until the dough is smooth. Place in a clean, floured bowl and cover with a damp cloth.

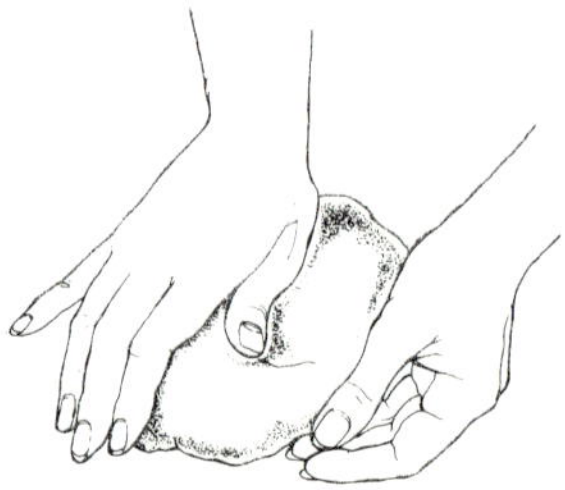

Leave in a warm place for about 1 hour until doubled in size. Turn out and knead again for a minute or so.

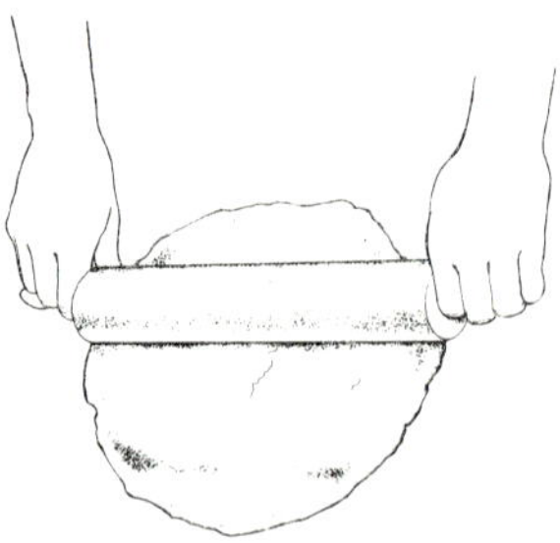

Divide the dough in two. Roll each piece out to a circular shape about 25 cm wide. Place on greased and floured baking trays. Preheat the oven to 230° C, 450° F/Gas 8.

Crimp or flute the edges slightly to help keep in the filling. Spread with the tomato sauce, sprinkle with the cheeses and then pour over a little oil. Bake near the bottom of the oven for about 5 minutes, then reduce the temperature to 200° C, 400° F/Gas 6 for a further 10 minutes.

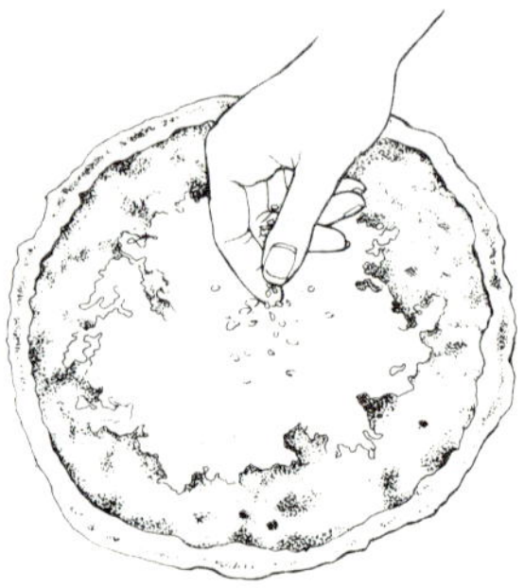

Salsa pizzaiola (tomato and garlic sauce)

Makes about 700 ml ($1\frac{1}{4}$ pints)

Fry 1 chopped onion in 2 tablespoons of olive oil until transparent. Add 3-4 cloves of chopped garlic and cook a further minute. Then stir in a $1\frac{1}{4}$-kg ($2\frac{1}{2}$-lb) can of plum tomatoes with their liquid, 2 tablespoons of tomato purée, 2 teaspoons of dried oregano, 1 teaspoon of dried basil, 1 bay leaf, 2 flat teaspoons of sugar, salt and a little freshly ground black pepper. Bring to the boil and then cook very gently for about 1 hour. Remove the bay leaf and check the seasoning. This sauce should be fairly thick and rough, but you could purée it if you wish.

To peel tomatoes quickly

Prick each tomato just once near the calyx with a sharp knife. Place in a large bowl and pour on boiling water. Leave for only 30 seconds, less if quite ripe; then remove from the water, and peel.

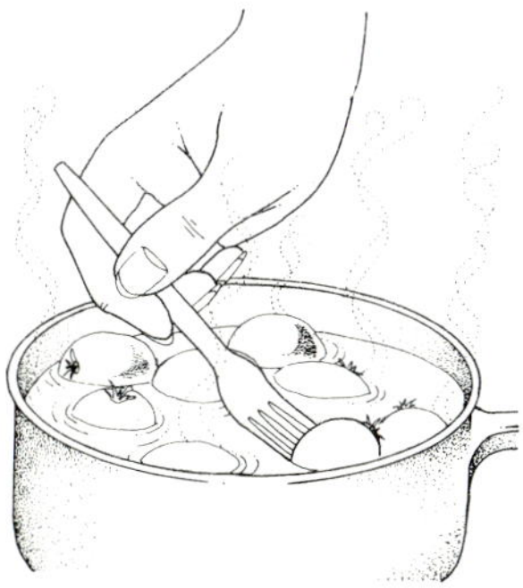

Pizza alla napoletana (Neapolitan pizza)

2 pizza bases, uncooked (see p. 34)
350 g (12 oz) peeled ripe or canned tomatoes
225 g (8 oz) Mozzarella, diced
8 anchovy fillets, chopped
4 teaspoons oregano or dried marjoram
pepper
olive oil

Place the bases on baking trays and top with the tomatoes, drained. Evenly cover with the diced cheese and the anchovy fillets. Sprinkle with the herbs and seasoning and a little oil. Bake as on p. 34.

Pizza ai funghi (mushroom pizza)

2 pizza bases, uncooked (see p. 34)
450 g (1 lb) mushrooms
2 cloves garlic, crushed
6-7 tablespoons olive oil
2 tablespoons chopped parsley
salt and black pepper

Place the bases on baking sheets. Wash the mushrooms and slice. Heat the oil and gently fry the garlic, mushrooms, parsley and seasoning for about 10 minutes. Spread over the pizza bases and bake as on p. 34.

Pizza de sarde (sardine pizza)

2 pizza bases, uncooked (see p. 34)
250 ml ($\frac{1}{2}$ pint) pizzaiola sauce (see p. 34)
6 fresh sardines or 2 cans, drained
salt and pepper
8-10 black olives
125 g (4 oz) Caciocavallo cheese, sliced
olive oil

Place the bases on baking sheets. Spread half the sauce over them evenly. Cut the sardines in half lengthwise and clean if fresh. Arrange on top of the pizza bases, with the cheese, olives and seasoning. Cover with the remaining sauce. Sprinkle with olive oil and bake as directed on p. 34.

Pizza con peperoni e prosciutto (pizza with peppers and ham)

2 pizza bases, uncooked (see p. 34)
165 ml ($\frac{1}{3}$ pint) pizzaiola sauce (see p. 34)
1 small green pepper
50 g (2 oz) smoked ham, diced
1 teaspoon dried oregano
25 g (1 oz) Parmesan
olive oil

Place the bases on baking sheets. Spread with the sauce. Seed, blanch and slice the pepper, and arrange on top with the ham. Sprinkle with the oregano and cheese and a little oil. Bake the pizzas as directed on p. 34.

Pizza con cozze (pizza with mussels)

2 pizza bases, uncooked (see p. 34)
6-7 tablespoons pizzaiola sauce (see p. 34)
450 g (1 pint) mussels, shelled
1 teaspoon dried basil or 2 teaspoons fresh basil, chopped
225 g (8 oz) Mozzarella
olive oil

Place the bases on baking sheets. Spread with the sauce and arrange the mussels, basil and cheese on top. Sprinkle the pizzas with olive oil and bake as directed on p. 34.

Pizza con cipolle e olive (pizza with onion and olives)

2 pizza bases, uncooked (see p. 34)
5-6 tablespoons olive oil
2 large onions, peeled and sliced
1$\frac{1}{2}$ dozen stuffed green olives, sliced
salt and pepper

Place the bases on baking sheets. Brush with a little oil. Heat the rest of the oil and fry the onions until translucent. Season, spread evenly over the pizzas and top with the olive slices and pepper. Bake as on p. 34.

Gnocchi and polenta

In both the north and south of Italy, gnocchi and polenta are what bread and potatoes are to many other regions of the world. They are the simple staples of the peasant folk, based on recipes from Roman times.

Gnocchi resemble small dumplings. They are eaten as a starter or as part of a main course. They can be made into any small interesting shape and poached, fried or baked. The original gnocchi, from Roman times, were made from a ground cereal into soufflé-like puddings. Now they are made from semolina or potatoes as well as from flour.

Polenta, which seems more popular in the north of Italy, is made of a fine or coarsely ground yellow cornmeal from maize. It produces a much heavier mixture, sometimes served hot like a porridge, or shaped, like gnocchi.

Gnocchi di semolina (gnocchi made with semolina)

Serves 4-6

500 ml (1 pint) milk
salt and pepper
pinch of nutmeg
100 g (4 oz) semolina
2 eggs
5-6 tablespoons Parmesan, grated
50-75 g (2-3 oz) butter and oil for frying

Place the milk in a large pan and season with salt, pepper and nutmeg. Bring to the boil and then slowly pour in all the semolina, stirring all the time with a wooden spoon. Continue cooking until the mixture is thick enough for the spoon to stand up. This can take up to 15-20 minutes. Allow to

◀ *Gnocchi alla piedmontese,* served with Béchamel sauce.

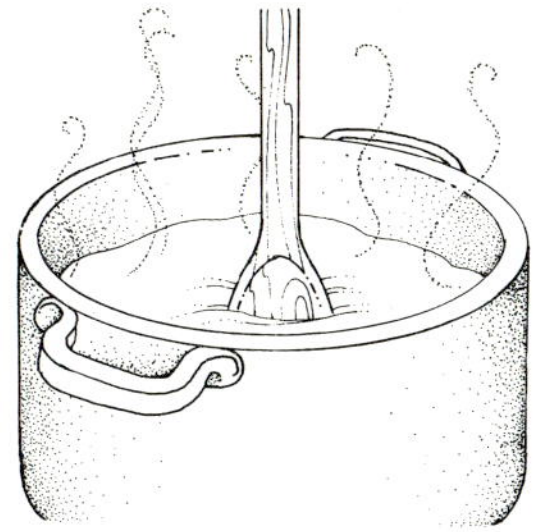

cool slightly and then beat in the eggs and half the cheese. Turn out onto a large plate, board or cold surface and leave until quite cold and firm. When nearly ready to serve cut the mix-

ture into 4-cm rounds or other shapes with a pastry cutter. Any extra mixture can be kneaded together, rolled and cut into more shapes.

Gently fry a few at a time in butter and oil until golden on both sides, and transfer to an ovenproof dish, sprinkling each layer with more cheese. Place under the grill for a few minutes before serving.

Alternative method

When the mixture is cool but not solid, shape a spoonful in floured hands into a ball.

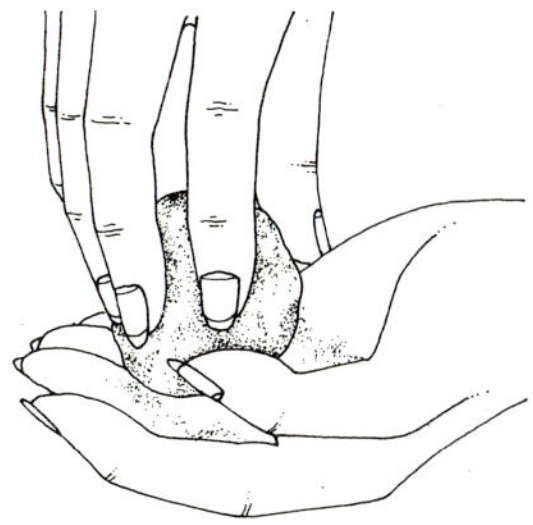

Drop several gnocchi balls into a pan of boiling salted water and simmer until they rise to the surface.

Remove with a draining spoon and place in an ovenproof dish, layered with butter and cheese. Bake at 200° C, 400° F/Gas 6 for about 20 minutes, until golden.

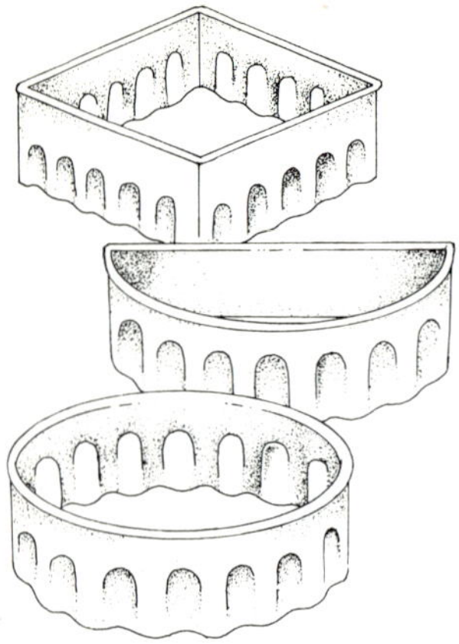

▲ Any pastry cutters can be used to cut both gnocchi and polenta. You can also use a small glass or tin lid, or when serving for a starter use very small sweet or biscuit cutters.

Gnocchi verdi (spinach gnocchi)

Serves 4-6

2×275-g (10-oz) packets frozen spinach or 675 g (1½ lb) fresh spinach
100 g (4 oz) butter
175 g (6 oz) Ricotta cheese or use 75 g (3 oz) cottage and cream cheese mixed together and sieved with 2 tablespoons cream
2 eggs
37 g (1½ oz) flour
75 g (3 oz) freshly grated Parmesan
salt
black pepper
pinch of nutmeg

Cook the frozen spinach as directed or blanch the fresh spinach, shredded, in boiling water. Then drain very well and squeeze dry. Fry gently in 50 g (2 oz) melted butter until beginning to stick to the pan. Add the Ricotta, or the cream and cheese mixture, and cook for 2-3 minutes. Transfer to a large mixing bowl and beat in the eggs, flour, cheese mixture, seasoning and 25 g (1 oz) of the Parmesan cheese. When smooth, chill for about 1 hour. To cook the gnocchi, bring a large pan of salted water to the boil. Shape the mixture, in floured hands, into small balls and cook several at a time in the simmering water for about 3 minutes, until they rise to the surface. Remove with a draining spoon and place in an ovenproof dish well greased with some of the butter. Sprinkle with Parmesan and place more of the cooked gnocchi on top until all the cheese and gnocchi are layered. Top with the remaining butter and grill until golden. Serve immediately.

Gnocchi alla romana (potato gnocchi)

Serves 4

900 g (2 lb) potatoes
225 g (8 oz) flour
salt
100 g (4 oz) Fontina cheese, thinly sliced
50 g (2 oz) butter
125 ml (¼ pint) tomato sauce (see p. 27)

Peel and boil the potatoes until soft. Mash them well until there are no lumps and then gradually work in the flour and salt. When the mixture is smooth but firm roll into small balls or leave until cold and cut into shapes. Layer in an ovenproof dish with the cheese and the butter and then top with the tomato sauce. Bake at 190° C, 375° F/Gas 5 for about 20 minutes.

Gnocchi alla piemontese (gnocchi fritters)

Serves 6

125 g (5 oz) semolina
500 ml (1 pint) milk
3 eggs
nutmeg, freshly grated
salt and pepper
50 g (2 oz) Parmesan, grated
50 g (2 oz) Emmenthal, finely diced
olive oil
2-3 tablespoons fine breadcrumbs
oil for frying
250 ml (½ pint) Béchamel sauce (see p. 30)

Heat the milk with the nutmeg and seasoning. Add the semolina gradually and bring to the boil, stirring all the time. When the spoon will stand up on its own in the mixture, stir in the Parmesan. Cool slightly before adding 2 eggs and the Emmenthal. Mix well and turn onto a cold surface. Brush lightly with oil, and smooth out to about 1 cm thick. When cold, cut into small diamond shapes. Lightly beat the remaining egg; dip the gnocchi in it and then roll them in egg and then into the breadcrumbs. When thoroughly coated, drop into hot deep fat and fry for 2-3 minutes, until crisp and golden. Drain on kitchen paper and serve with a creamy Béchamel sauce and extra grated Parmesan cheese.

Polentina valtellina (polenta and cheese pudding)

Serves 4

225 g (8 oz) buckwheat or wheatmeal flour
37 g (1½ oz) fine cornmeal
salt and pepper
125 g (4-5 oz) butter
100 g (4 oz) Taleggio cheese, or Mozzarella or Bel Paese, cut into thin strips

Mix the flour and meal together with the seasoning. Bring just over 750 ml (1½ pints) of water to the boil and then gradually sprinkle on the mixture, stirring with a wooden spoon all the time. Cook gently for about 1 hour, stirring occasionally to prevent sticking. Then add the butter, stirring until completely mixed in, and then stir in the cheeses. Mix well for another 5 minutes, turn into a serving dish and serve really hot.

Polenta alla lodigiana (polenta fritters)

Makes about 12 fritters

250 ml (½ pint) milk
salt
50 g (2 oz) cornmeal
100 g (4 oz) Gruyère cheese
flour
1 egg, beaten
1-2 tablespoons fine breadcrumbs
50 g (2 oz) butter
1 tablespoon oil

Heat the milk, with a little salt, until boiling. Gradually stir in the cornmeal and cook for about 30 minutes, stirring occasionally, until thick. Then turn out onto a wetted cold surface, and leave until cool. Cut into small circles or fingers. Cut the cheese into thin slices the same shape. Sandwich 2 pieces of polenta and 1 piece of cheese together. Dip lightly in flour, then into the egg. Finally coat in crumbs and fry in the hot butter and oil. When browned, drain and serve immediately.

Polenta ai funghi (polenta with mushroom sauce)

Serves 6

350 g (12 oz) cornmeal
salt
225 g (8 oz) mushrooms
a little olive oil
25 g (1 oz) chopped bacon or ham
1 carrot, finely chopped
1 small onion, chopped
75 g (3 oz) sausage meat
2 tablespoons tomato sauce or puréed tomatoes
50 g (2 oz) butter
50 g (2 oz) Parmesan, grated

Cook the cornmeal as described for *polenta valtellina*, cooking in 1¼ litres (2½ pints) of water. Spread out and leave to cool. Fry the chopped mushrooms in oil with the bacon or ham, carrot, onion and sausage meat for about 15 minutes. Stir in the tomato sauce, mix well and season to taste. Cut the polenta into rounds and place a layer in the base of a well buttered ovenproof dish. Cover with a little of the sauce, a little butter and a light sprinkling of cheese. Repeat the layers until all the polenta and sauce are used up, and bake at 220° C, 425° F/Gas 7 for about 10 minutes, until golden.

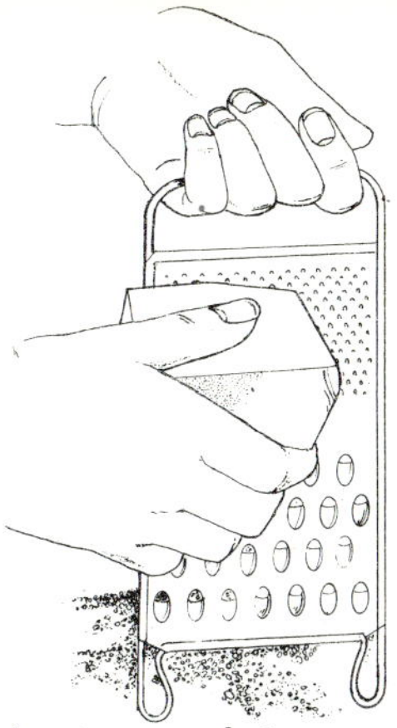

Polenta napoletana (polenta with spiced sausages)

Serves 4-6

350 g (12 oz) cornmeal
450 g (1 lb) cotechino (see p. 84) or spicy sausages
50 g (2 oz) Parmesan, grated
50 g (2 oz) butter
350 g (12 oz) Mozzarella, thinly sliced
salt and pepper

Prepare the polenta as described for *polenta valtellina* and pour into a deep wetted dish. Leave until cold. Prick the sausages and fry gently until most of the fat runs out and they are golden. Cool, skin and slice. Add 25 g (1 oz) of the Parmesan to the pan the sausages were cooked in and mix well. Cut the polenta into thin slices and place a layer in the base of an ovenproof dish greased with a little of the sausage fat and cheese. Brush the polenta with sausage fat, and cover with a layer of Mozzarella and sausage meat. Repeat, finishing with a layer of cheese. Dot with butter, and bake at 190° C, 375° F/Gas 5 for 30 minutes.

Rice dishes

Every rice-growing country has its own special rice dish. In Italy it is the risotto, which can be enormously varied but still requires its own unique way of cooking.

Italy is the biggest rice-growing country in Europe, but it produces a very different rice to the ones most people know best. Italian rice has rounded grains, very similar to pudding rice but slightly larger.

The Italian method of cooking rice is the heart of a good risotto: long gentle cooking in a well-flavoured stock. There is sometimes argument about the need to wash it first, but if the quality of the rice is good enough this should not be necessary.

To boil rice

Bring a very large pan of salted water to the boil and pour in the rice in a steady stream. Bring back to the boil and stir once or twice to separate the grains. Leave to simmer uncovered and undisturbed for about 15 minutes. Then test in exactly the same way as for pasta (see p. 26). The rice should be still just firm in the centre of the grain. Drain, and toss in a little butter or oil. To keep warm, place in a sieve over a pan of simmering water.

Allow about 75 g (3 oz) of uncooked rice per person for a main dish.

To cook rice the Italian way

For a risotto the rice should be gently fried in a *soffritto* or *battuto* – a finely chopped mixture of onion, garlic and parsley which has already been lightly fried to bring out the flavours. Then a good fresh stock is added in small quantities as the rice swells and dries out. However it should not be allowed to dry out completely, and in fact an Italian risotto should be much moister than Spanish or Indian rice dishes. This may seem too soft and mushy for some tastes; but it is in this type of dish that you will notice the advantages of using Italian rice. It will not break down nearly as easily as other types of rice, and even when the risotto seems mushy the rice will still have enough bite to it. Never strain a risotto.

Riso ai quattro formaggi (rice with four cheeses)

Serves 3-4

225 g (8 oz) rice
salt
37 g (1½ oz) Provolone cheese
37 g (1½ oz) Bel Paese
37 g (1½ oz) Gruyère
75 g (3 oz) Parmesan, grated
50 g (2 oz) ham or tongue
butter

Cook the rice in boiling salted water as described above, until almost tender (it will have more cooking in the oven, so it is better to undercook). Chop the cheeses, except the Parmesan, which should be grated, and dice the ham or tongue. Mix together with half the Parmesan. Put a

◀ *Riso ai quattro formaggi:*

▼ Some rice types. From left to right: round grain; brown rice; Italian rice; medium grain (Carolina); long grain (Patna).

layer of cooked rice in the base of a buttered ovenproof dish. Cover with a layer of cheese and ham and flakes of butter. Continue, ending with a layer of rice. Cover this with the remaining butter and Parmesan. Place the dish in a *bain-marie*, or tin of hot water, in the oven at 200° C, 400° F/ Gas 6 for about 25 minutes. The top should be golden and crisp but the pan of water will keep the rice moist. This dish can be served with meat sauce, but is rich enough to be enjoyed on its own.

Suppli al telefono (rice and cheese croquettes)

These crisp-coated and soft-centred mouthfuls are a very good way of using up plain boiled rice, or the remains of a simple risotto.

Serves 4

500 g (18 oz) cooked rice or risotto or 175 g (6 oz) uncooked rice
salt and pepper
2 eggs
100 g (4 oz) Mozzarella or Bel Paese cheese
75 g (3 oz) fine breadcrumbs
oil for frying

If using plain previously boiled rice add just a little seasoning. If it is freshly cooked, drain well. Lightly beat together the eggs and mix with the rice. Cut the cheese into 1-cm cubes. Take a spoonful of rice mixture and flatten it in the palm of your hand. Put a piece of cheese in the middle and mould the rice

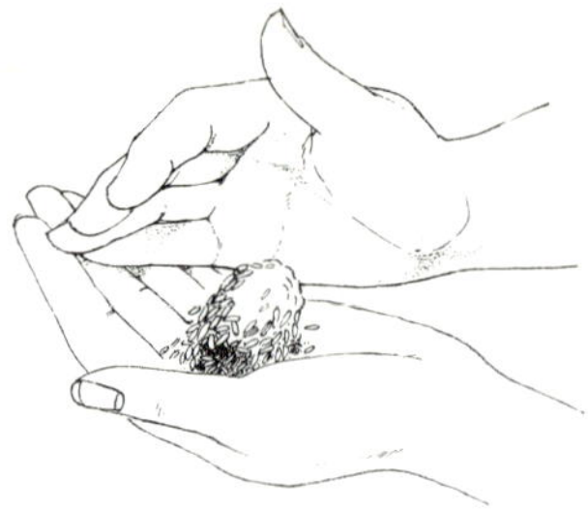

around it. Roll into a ball and then coat lightly in the breadcrumbs. Fry in hot oil for 4-5 minutes, until crisp and golden, and drain on kitchen paper. Place in an ovenproof dish in the oven to keep warm while cooking the rest. Serve immediately so the cheese in the middle is just melting.

The same croquettes can be made with other fillings: chopped ham, preferably Parma ham; stoned olives; chopped truffles; or small shrimps.

Risi e bisi (rice and peas)

Serves 4

775 ml ($1\frac{1}{2}$ pints) chicken stock
62 g ($2\frac{1}{2}$ oz) butter
1 small onion, chopped
675 g ($1\frac{1}{2}$ lb) fresh peas in their pods
275 g (10 oz) white rice
100 g (4 oz) smoked ham, chopped
37 g ($1\frac{1}{2}$ oz) Parmesan, freshly grated

Bring the stock to the boil and leave simmering. Melt 37 g ($1\frac{1}{2}$ oz) of butter in a heavy-based pan and cook the onion until transparent. Add the peas, rice and ham and cook until coated in butter. Add half the stock and simmer uncovered until it is all absorbed. Then add the rest of the stock and cook, stirring, until this too has been absorbed and the rice and peas are tender. Stir in the remaining butter and the cheese. Serve immediately.

Risotto alla toscana (Tuscan risotto)

Serves 4-6

2-3 tablespoons olive oil
50 g (2 oz) butter
1 small onion, thinly sliced
1 small carrot, finely chopped
1 stick celery, diced
225 g (8 oz) minced beef
100 g (4 oz) calf's liver, chopped
1-2 chicken livers, chopped
6 tablespoons red wine
2 teaspoons tomato purée
1 litre (2-$2\frac{1}{2}$ pints) stock
salt and pepper
grated nutmeg
450 g (1 lb) rice
50 g (2 oz) Parmesan, grated

Heat the oil and half the butter and gently fry the chopped vegetables until golden. Add the beef and livers and stir until brown; then add the wine. Cook until partly reduced. Dilute the purée in a little hot stock and add to the pan with the salt, pepper and nutmeg. Cover and simmer gently for about 30 minutes. Then gradually pour the rice into the pan and stir until well coated and almost transparent. Add a little of the stock, cook until absorbed, and then add more. Continue until the rice is creamy but not overcooked. Stir in the remaining butter and the cheese and serve immediately.

Risotto alla milanese (risotto with saffron and beef marrow)

Serves 4-6

1 litre (2 pints) stock
75 g (3 oz) butter
1 small onion, chopped
37 g ($1\frac{1}{2}$ oz) chopped beef marrow, uncooked (optional)
350 g (12 oz) rice
4-5 tablespoons dry white wine
pinch of powdered saffron (or turmeric) or a few saffron threads
4-5 tablespoons Parmesan, grated

Keep the stock simmering while you heat half the butter and lightly fry the onion. Stir in the marrow and the rice and cook until the marrow is coated and translucent. Pour in the wine and cook until reduced. Then cook as described for *risi e bisi*, adding the stock gradually. The saffron powder can be added directly to the pan of cooking rice but the strands need to be soaked in the hot stock to bring out their colour. Remove the strands before adding the stock to the rice. When the rice is creamy but still firm add the remaining butter and the grated cheese, and stir well before serving.

Risotto con scampi (rice with prawns)

Serves 4-6

450 g (1 lb) prawns, unshelled
450 g (1 lb) fish trimmings and heads
3-4 tablespoons dry white wine
small onion, chopped
1 carrot, chopped
sprig of fresh parsley
1 bay leaf
75 g (3 oz) butter
1 clove garlic, crushed
350 g (12 oz) rice
50 g (2 oz) Parmesan, grated
salt and pepper

Shell the prawns, keeping the shells, and remove the black vein down the backs with a sharp knife. Put the shells, fish trimmings and heads and the wine, onion, carrot, parsley and bay leaf into a large pan with about $1\frac{1}{2}$ litres (3 pints) of water. Bring to the boil and simmer for 30 minutes. Sieve, extracting all the juices from the fish and vegetables. Melt 37 g ($1\frac{1}{2}$ oz) of butter in a large saucepan and fry the garlic and prawns for 2 to 3 minutes, until the prawns are tender and pink. Keep the prawns warm. Add the rice to the pan and toss in the hot butter until the rice is translucent. Add half the stock and cook gently until it is absorbed. Add the rest of the stock and cook until just tender. Gently stir in the prawns and reheat quickly. Stir in the rest of the butter and the cheese and serve immediately.

Riso al limone (rice with lemon)

Serves 4

salt
225 g (8 oz) Italian rice, uncooked
25 g (1 oz) butter
3 eggs
75 g (3 oz) Parmesan, grated
3 tablespoons lemon juice
salt and black pepper

Fill a very large pan with plenty of salted water. Bring to the boil and add the rice. Cook as described for *risi e bisi*, and when just tender, drain. Melt the butter in a saucepan and add the rice. Beat the eggs together in a bowl and then beat in the cheese, lemon juice and seasoning. Stir this mixture into the rice and cook over a very low heat for 3-4 minutes, stirring occasionally. Serve while the rice is still creamy.

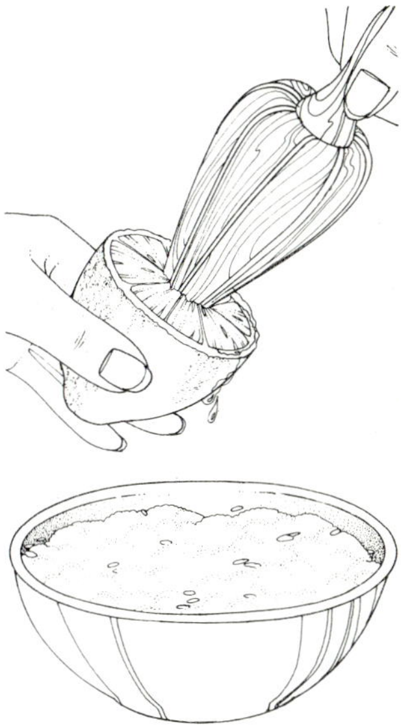

► Squeeze small amounts of lemon juice straight onto the food as required.

Vegetable cookery

When vegetables are served as dishes in their own right they seem more likely to get the respect they really deserve. The Italians serve them often as a first course, or part of the antipasta, raw or very gently cooked wherever possible, and delightfully flavoured with herbs, sauces and many other seasonings.

Zucchini ripieni (stuffed courgettes with tomato sauce)

Serves 4 as a starter, 2 as a main course

4 small courgettes
1-2 tablespoons olive oil
$\frac{1}{2}$ onion, peeled and finely chopped
1 clove garlic, crushed
100 g (4 oz) minced beef
25 g (1 oz) Parma or smoked ham
1 tablespoon fresh white breadcrumbs
2 tablespoons Parmesan, grated
$\frac{1}{4}$ teaspoon dried oregano
salt and freshly ground black pepper
1 small egg, lightly beaten
125 ml ($\frac{1}{4}$ pint) tomato sauce (see p. 27)

Wash the courgettes, trim the ends and slice lengthwise. With a teaspoon scoop out the centres and chop or mash them. Heat the oil and fry the onion and garlic until golden. Add the courgette pulp and the beef and simmer for about 5 minutes. Then mix in the chopped ham, breadcrumbs, a little cheese, oregano and seasoning. When well mixed allow to cool slightly before adding the egg. Spoon into the courgette shells. Spread most of the tomato sauce in the base of an ovenproof dish. Arrange the courgettes on top, sprinkle with the remaining sauce and cheese and a little oil. Bake at 190° C, 375° F/Gas 5 for approximately 30 minutes. This tasty dish is cooked when the cheese on top is golden and bubbling. Take out and serve.

Carciofi ripieni di ricotta (stuffed artichokes)

Serves 4

4 small young artichokes
juice of 1 lemon
50 g (2 oz) butter
175 g (6 oz) Ricotta cheese or cottage cheese
1 small egg, beaten
2 tablespoons Parmesan, grated
50-75 g (2-3 oz) Italian salame, diced
salt and black pepper
2 tablespoons fine breadcrumbs

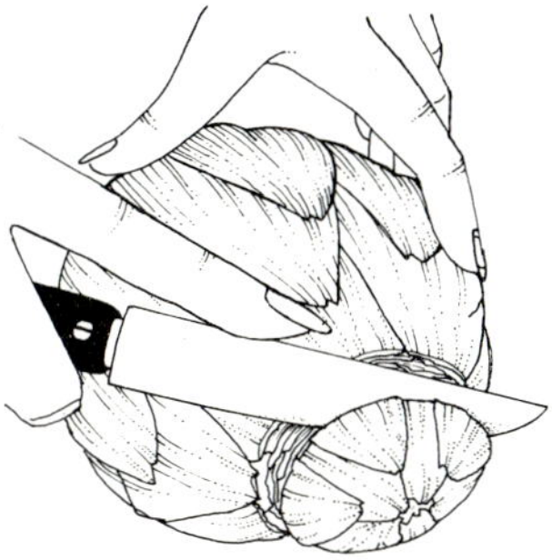

To prepare the artichokes, remove any rough outer leaves and cut the rest down by about 2cm with scissors or a sharp knife. Dip the tip

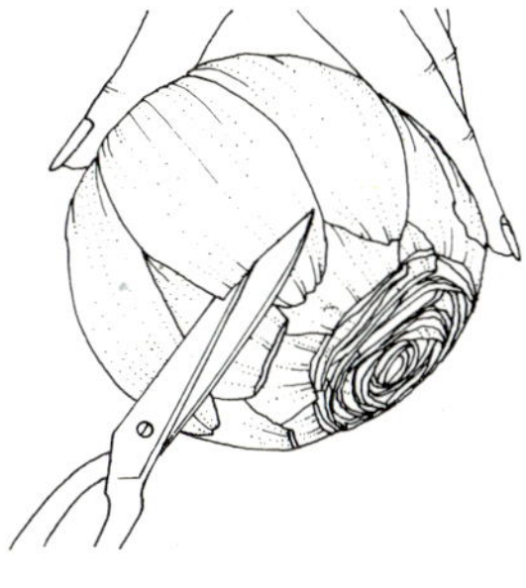

of the leaves into lemon juice. Trim the bases so they stand upright; then place in a pan of boiling salted water and bring back to the boil. Simmer for about 15 minutes; drain; and cool. Meanwhile blend together the butter, Ricotta, egg, Parmesan and salame. Season lightly.

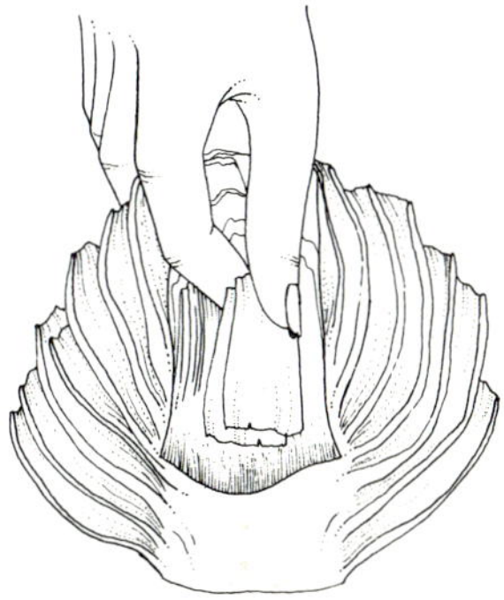

When the artichokes are cool, spread the leaves out so you can remove the very tiny ones from the middle and the hairy 'choke' underneath. This is the inedible part.

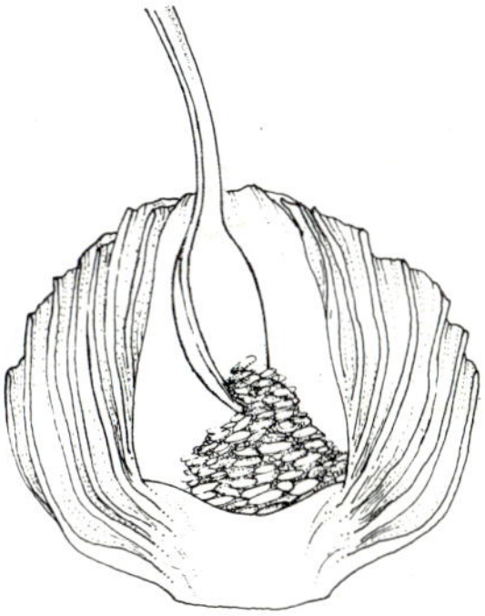

Spoon in the cheese filling and sprinkle with some of the breadcrumbs. Reshape, place in an ovenproof dish and sprinkle with the remaining breadcrumbs. Bake for about 15 minutes, covered with a lid or foil, and serve immediately.

Verzada (cabbage with pork sausages)

Serves 4

1 medium cabbage, preferably white, about 675 g (1½ lb)
a little butter or oil
75 g (3 oz) belly of pork or streaky bacon, chopped
1 small onion, sliced
2 tablespoons white wine vinegar
salt and black pepper
6 small spicy pork sausages, chopped

Trim the cabbage, discarding the outside leaves; then finely shred it. Melt the butter and fry the pork or bacon and the onion until golden. Add the shredded cabbage and toss in the mixture until well coated. Add the vinegar, seasoning and sausages and cover. Simmer gently for about 50 minutes, stirring from time to time.

Zuppa di fagioli (white bean soup)

This popular Tuscan soup can be served with an Italian version of croutons, topped with cheese.

Serves 4

225 g (8 oz) white haricot beans, soaked overnight
olive oil
1 clove garlic, crushed
1 small onion, chopped
1 small ham bone
sprig of parsley and thyme
salt and pepper

For croutons:

4 small slices or rounds of bread
25 g (1 oz) butter
50 g (2 oz) Parmesan, grated

Drain the beans. Heat 2 tablespoons of oil in a large saucepan and gently fry the garlic and onion. Add the bone, herbs, seasonings and the beans, and enough water to cover. Bring to the boil and simmer for about 1½ hours. When the beans are tender remove the ham bone, and sieve or liquidize half the beans with some of the liquid. Return to the pan and keep hot. Meanwhile spread the bread with the butter, sprinkle with the cheese and bake in the oven for about 15 minutes at 200° C, 400° F/Gas 6, until crisp and golden. Place the bread in the base of individual bowls or a soup tureen and pour the soup on this. Return to the oven for a further 10 minutes before serving.

Peperoni imbottiti (baked stuffed peppers)

Serves 4

4 small green peppers
3 tablespoons soft breadcrumbs
3-4 anchovy fillets
2 teaspoons capers, chopped
1 tablespoon pine nuts
1 tablespoon sultanas
salt and pepper
1 tablespoon parsley, chopped
olive oil

Cut the stalk off the peppers and remove the seeds with a teaspoon. Place the peppers under a hot grill or over a gas flame until slightly blistered all over. When cooled a little, rub off the skins and arrange the peppers upright in an ovenproof dish. Mix together the crumbs, fillets, capers, nuts, sultanas, seasoning and parsley and moisten with a little oil. Spoon the mixture into the peppers; replace the tops, and bake at 180° C, 350° F/Gas 4 for about 40 minutes, until tender.

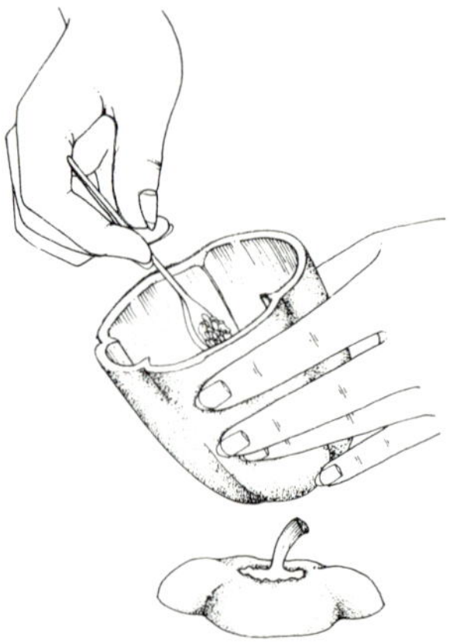

Uova alla fiorentina (eggs florentine)

Serves 4

225 g (8 oz) cooked spinach
25 g (1 oz) butter
salt and black pepper
2 tablespoons Parmesan, grated
250 ml (½ pint) Béchamel sauce (see p. 30)
4 eggs
2 tablespoons fine breadcrumbs

Squeeze the spinach as dry as possible. Place in a pan with the butter, seasoning and 1 tablespoon of Parmesan. When well mixed, place in the base of an ovenproof serving dish or four individual dishes, and keep warm. Heat the sauce. Poach the eggs very lightly in boiling salted water and place on top of the spinach. Pour the sauce over and top with the remaining cheese and the breadcrumbs. Place under the grill for about 5 minutes to brown off, or in the oven at 190° C, 375° F/ Gas 5 for about 15 minutes, until golden.

Cipolle di napoli (onions in tomato sauce)

Serves 4

8 medium mild onions
2 cloves garlic, crushed
3-4 tablespoons olive oil
salt and black pepper
2 teaspoons fresh thyme or 1 teaspoon dried thyme, chopped
125 ml ($\frac{1}{4}$ pint) tomato sauce (see p. 27)
2 tablespoons Marsala, or sweet sherry or white wine

Peel the onions, without cutting off too much flesh at each end. Place in a shallow ovenproof dish and sprinkle with the garlic, oil, seasoning, and thyme. Cover, and bake at 190° C, 375° F/Gas 5 for about 1 hour, or until the onions are just tender. Mix the tomato sauce and Marsala together and pour over. Cook for a further 20 minutes uncovered. Serve as a vegetable or as a light dish on its own.

Melanzane alla parmigiana (aubergine and Parmesan bake)

Serves 4

3 large aubergines
salt
olive oil
675 g (1½ lb) tomatoes, peeled and chopped
2 teaspoons basil, chopped
75 g (3 oz) Parmesan, grated
175 g (6 oz) Mozzarella, sliced
2 hard-boiled eggs, sliced

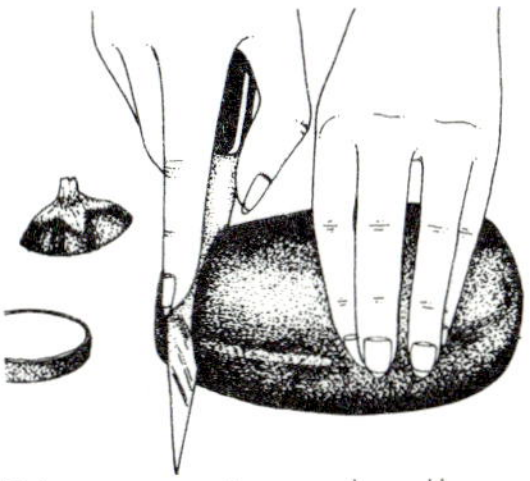

Trim, peel and slice the aubergines. Arrange on a large plate and sprinkle generously with salt. Leave

for about 20 minutes for the liquid to run out – this removes their bitterness. Drain and dry well. Heat a little oil and fry the slices until golden on both sides. Remove the slices, and add the tomatoes and basil to the pan and simmer until puréed. Arrange the aubergine in layers in an ovenproof serving dish with the tomato sauce, Parmesan, Mozzarella and egg slices, ending with a layer of aubergine covered with Parmesan. Bake for about 35 minutes at 190° C, 375° F/Gas 5, until crisp and golden on top.

Broccoli al crudo (broccoli braised in wine and garlic)

Serves 4

675 g (1½ lb) broccoli heads
salt and black pepper
3-4 tablespoons olive oil
2 cloves garlic, crushed
165 ml ($\frac{1}{3}$ pint) dry white wine
2 tablespoons double cream

Wash and trim the broccoli heads. Divide into small pieces or florets. Heat the oil in a large saucepan and gently fry the garlic until golden. Add the broccoli, seasoning and half the wine and simmer gently until tender. Add the remaining wine, bring to the boil and check seasoning. Add the cream and boil for 2 minutes, until slightly thickened. Serve immediately.

▼ To crush garlic quickly and simply, peel off the outer skin and press it down on a wooden board with a wide-bladed knife. Sprinkle with salt to prevent slipping.

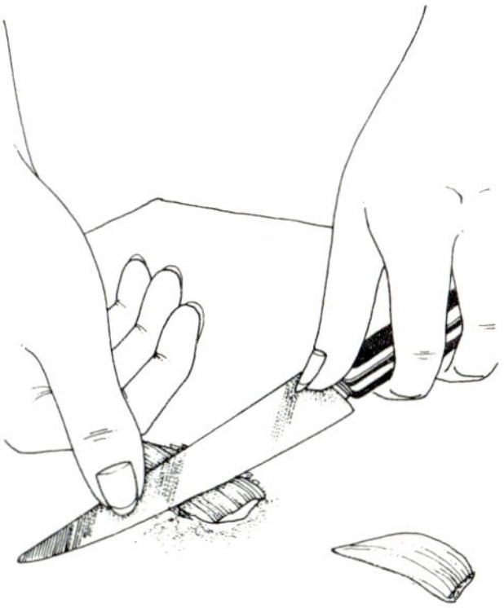

Meat dishes

Although the greatest original features of Italian cooking are generally held to be other foods such as pasta, many of the meat dishes traditional to Italy deserve to be far more highly regarded than they sometimes are. They are distinguished both for their varied use of the more expensive meats, like veal, and for clever ways of making the cheaper cuts go further.

Although in Italy the cattle, in particular, are put to better use as a source of excellent cheese rather than meat, Italian cooking is not without some outstanding meat specialities. Excellent veal, or *vitello,* is frequently consumed, as too is *vitellone,* its older equivalent. To produce *vitellone,* the cattle are kept idle for three years and fed on milk, so producing best-quality beef used for steaks and roasts. Very good pork, too, is reared, especially around Bologna, and the local *porchetta,* or sucking pig, is renowned. Much kid, goat and venison and other game are frequently eaten, as is chicken, which is both plentiful and cheap.

Simple roasts and grills, in Italian cooking, are often shown off by clever use of herbs, such as oregano (left) and parsley (right), and wine or Marsala.

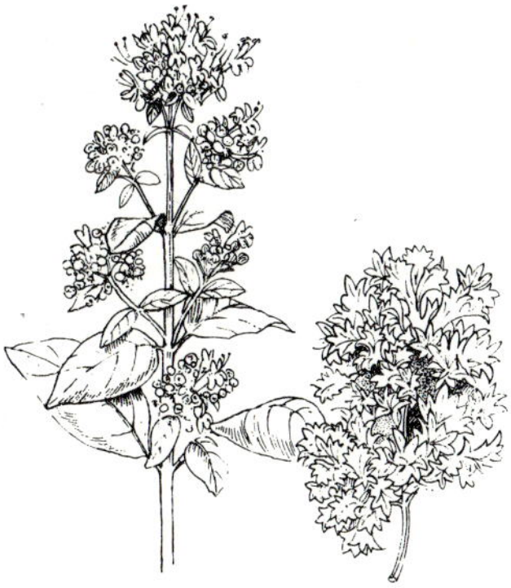

◀ A selection of meat dishes. Left to right: *cosciotto di agnello arrosto; pollo alla cacciatora; zampa di vitello alla toscana.*

▲ Chop herbs using the knife with a rocking motion and keeping its point on the board.

Cosciotte di agnello arrosto (pot-roasted lamb with herbs)

Serves 4-6

leg of lamb, about $1\frac{1}{3}$ kg (3 lb)
1 tablespoon parsley, chopped
2 cloves garlic, crushed
$\frac{1}{2}$ tablespoon chopped marjoram and thyme, fresh, or 1 teaspoon, dried
100 g (4 oz) Parma ham, finely chopped
salt and black pepper
50 g (2 oz) butter
1 tablespoon oil
165 ml ($\frac{1}{3}$ pint) dry white wine and water mixed (use as great a proportion of wine as you feel you can afford)

Wipe the meat and place in a deep roasting tin. Mix together the herbs, garlic, ham and seasoning. Press this mixture over the skin of the lamb. Add the oil and heat through; then brown the meat on the underside. Cover, with foil if you have no lid, before placing in the oven at 220° C, 425° F/Gas 7 for about 20 minutes. Add the wine and water; cover the meat; and return to the oven at 190° C, 375° F/Gas 5, for a further 30 minutes, basting occasionally. Cook for an extra 10-15 minutes if you don't like lamb pink.

Zampa di vitello alla toscana (calf's foot Tuscan style)

Serves 4

4 calf's or pig's trotters
salt and pepper
1 large onion, chopped
1 stick celery, diced
1 carrot, sliced
25 g (1 oz) butter
2-3 tablespoons olive oil
4 tablespoons tomato purée
1 tablespoon parsley, chopped
pinch ground cinnamon
2 tablespoons Parmesan, grated

Wash the trotters well and boil in a large pan of seasoned water with half of the onion, the celery, and the carrot for about 2 hours, until the meat is tender. When cool enough, remove the meat from the bones and cut it into pieces. (Keep any surplus stock for soups.) Heat the butter and oil and fry the remaining onions until golden; then add the meat and a little of the stock. Season, and simmer until the stock is reduced. Gradually stir in the purée with 125 ml ($\frac{1}{4}$ pint) more stock; and simmer, stirring frequently, until well blended. Finally stir in the parsley and cinnamon and sprinkle with cheese before serving.

Cima alla genovese (cold stuffed breast of veal)

Serves 6-8

3 slices white bread
125 ml ($\frac{1}{4}$ pint) milk
25 g (1 oz) butter
2 small onions, chopped
100 g (4 oz) minced pork
100 g (4 oz) minced veal
100 g (4 oz) minced fatty pork or belly of pork
1 small calf's sweetbread
4 tablespoons Parmesan, grated
$\frac{1}{4}$ teaspoon each dried thyme and marjoram
salt and black pepper
1 egg, beaten
50 g (2 oz) shelled pistachio nuts
100-g (4-oz) packet frozen peas
$1\frac{3}{4}$-$2\frac{1}{4}$ kg ($4\frac{1}{2}$ lb) breast of veal or 2 small pieces, boned
3 hard-boiled eggs
2 cloves garlic
bay leaf
sprig of parsley
2 litres (3-4 pints) chicken stock

Soak the bread in the milk. Blanch the sweetbread for 10 minutes and finely chop. Melt the butter and fry half the onions in it until cooked but not browned. Place the onions in a large bowl and mix in the pork, veal and fat and the sweetbread, the cheese, herbs, seasoning and egg. Mix well and then beat in the squeezed bread, the nuts and the thawed peas.

If using 1 large breast of veal, boned, batten this out with a rolling pin until as flat as possible and then spread the stuffing mixture evenly all over it.

Arrange the eggs in the middle and then roll up the veal carefully from the long side. Tie firmly at intervals

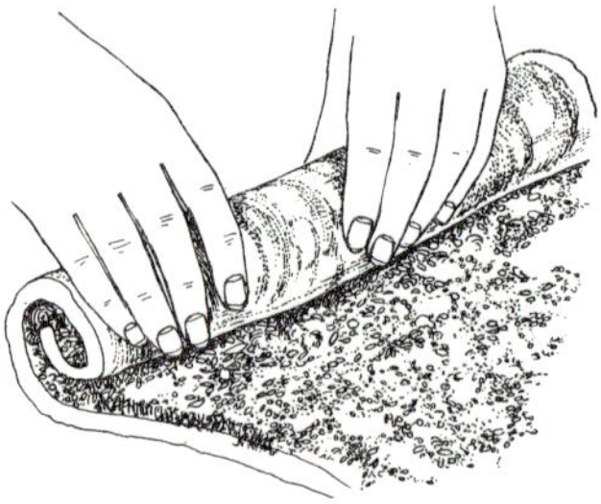

with string. If using 2 smaller pieces of veal, sew the outside edges together with strong cotton and then stuff the centre before rolling.

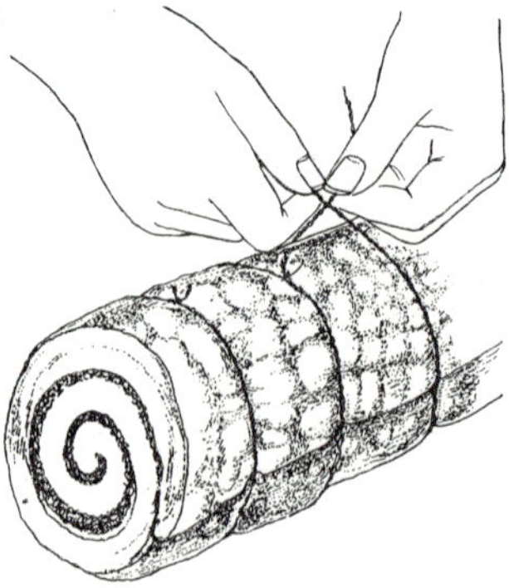

Place the veal bones if you have them, with the remaining onion and the garlic, bay leaf, parsley and seasonings, in a large pan. Place the veal on top and pour on enough stock to come at least halfway up the sides of the meat. Simmer, covered, for about $1\frac{1}{2}$ hours or braise at 190° C, 375° F/Gas 5. Check the liquid and baste the meat occasionally. Top up with extra water if necessary.

When the veal is tender, transfer it to a large plate and leave to drain and cool for several hours. Serve chilled.

Keep the cooking liquid for other veal, beef or chicken casseroles or soups.

Vitello alla marengo (veal in white wine and tomato sauce)

A popular family dish in Italy, which is often made with chicken or pork instead of veal.

Serves 4-6

675 g ($1\frac{1}{2}$ lb) breast or loin of veal
oil
1 onion, chopped
salt and pepper
1 flat tablespoon flour
165 ml ($\frac{1}{3}$ pint) white wine
165 ml ($\frac{1}{3}$ pint) beef or veal stock
450 g (1 lb) tomatoes, peeled and chopped
1 clove garlic, crushed
bay leaf
pinch dried chopped thyme
25 g (1 oz) butter
175 g (6 oz) button mushrooms
1 tablespoon parsley, chopped
4 slices bread, quartered

Cut the veal into cubes and lightly fry in oil until browned. Add the onion and seasoning. Evenly sprinkle on the flour, stirring all the time to blend in. Add the wine and stock, stirring until well blended, over a low heat. Add the tomatoes, garlic, bay leaf and thyme and bring to the boil. Stir until smooth and then cover. Simmer gently for about 40 minutes, or transfer to the oven and cook for 1 hour at 190° C, 375° F/Gas 5. Fry the mushrooms in the butter. Add the mushrooms to the veal and return it to the oven for a further 10 minutes or continue simmering. Before serving, sprinkle with parsley and top with the bread fried in oil until crisp.

Fried bread croutons make a quick accompaniment to casseroles, although Italians would serve polenta.

Polpette alla salvia (meatballs with sage)
Serves 4
450 g (1 lb) minced beef
50 g (2 oz) Italian sausages, skinned
2 tablespoons Parmesan, grated
salt and black pepper
pinch of grated nutmeg
1 teaspoon dried chopped sage
1 egg, beaten
25 g (1 oz) butter
flour
oil

Mix together the beef, sausages, cheese, seasonings, nutmeg, sage and egg thoroughly until well blended. Melt the butter and blend that in. In floured hands, shape the mixture into 3-cm-diameter meatballs and fry in hot oil for about 8 minutes, turning frequently, until golden and firm. Drain on kitchen paper while cooking the rest and serve with tomato or Béchamel sauce (see p. 27 or p. 30).

Scaloppine al marsala (sautéed escalopes of veal in Marsala sauce)
Serves 4
4 veal escalopes
salt and black pepper
a little flour
1 tablespoon butter
2 tablespoons olive oil
3-4 tablespoons Marsala
125 ml ($\frac{1}{4}$ pint) chicken stock
1 tablespoon double cream

Prepare the escalopes as described on p. 58. Then season lightly and dip in the flour. Gently fry in the hot butter and oil until golden on both sides. Transfer to a plate and keep warm. Drain off any excess fat from the pan and pour in the Marsala and stock. Bring to the boil and cook until well reduced. Then stir in the cream. Add the escalopes and simmer for a further 3-5 minutes before serving.

Pollo alla cacciatora (chicken with olive and anchovy sauce)
Serves 4
4 portions of chicken
salt and black pepper
2 tablespoons olive oil
1 small onion, diced
2 cloves garlic, crushed
5-6 tablespoons dry white wine
1 tablespoon white wine vinegar
5-6 tablespoons chicken stock
pinch dried oregano
1 bay leaf
25 g (1 oz) black olives
2-3 anchovy fillets

Season the chicken portions lightly with salt and pepper and fry in the hot oil. When golden on both sides, transfer to another dish and keep warm. Lightly fry the onion and garlic in some of the remaining oil and then stir in the wine and vinegar. Bring to the boil and simmer for about 5 minutes. Add the chicken stock, herbs and bay leaf and cover. Simmer gently for about 25 minutes or until the chicken is cooked. Meanwhile cut the olives off the stones in tiny thin slivers. Rinse the anchovy fillets in cold water, and dry and chop them. Add both these to the sauce for the last 5 minutes, and remove the lid if necessary to reduce the sauce before serving.

Osso buco (braised veal knuckles)

This Italian speciality contains not only tender meat, but juicy marrow from the centre of the bones. You may need to order this cut of veal from your butcher well in advance. Be sure to explain what you need it for so that he can prepare the meat correctly and give you as much marrow as possible.

Serves 4-6

25 g (1 oz) butter
1 small onion, chopped
1 carrot, chopped
3 cloves garlic, crushed
$1\frac{1}{3}$ kg (3 lb) knuckle of veal (ask the butcher to cut it into 4 or 8 pieces)
salt and black pepper
olive oil
125 ml ($\frac{1}{4}$ pint) dry white wine
125 ml ($\frac{1}{4}$ pint) stock
pinch of basil and thyme
2 bay leaves
small can of tomatoes
$1\frac{1}{2}$ teaspoons grated lemon peel
2 tablespoons chopped parsley

Melt the butter in a large heavy-based pan and gently fry the onion and carrot and a clove of garlic in it until golden. Transfer to an ovenproof dish.

Meanwhile lightly tie the meat and bone together with strong cotton.

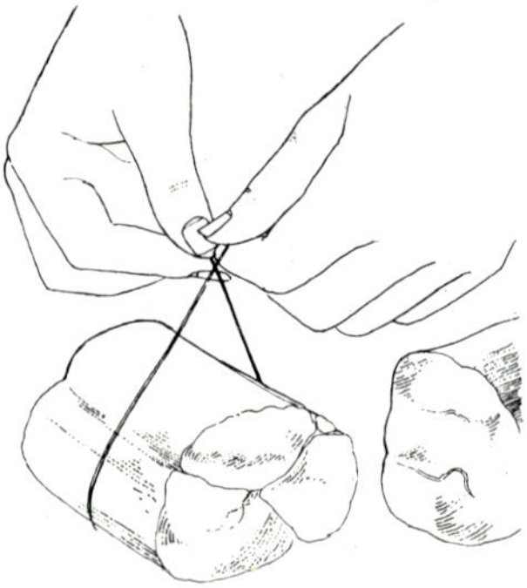

Season the meat and fry in the remaining butter with a little oil, turning until golden all over. Place in the pan with the vegetables.

Stir the wine, stock, herbs, tomatoes and a little seasoning into the frying pan. Bring to the boil and pour over the meat and vegetables. Cover

and bake at 190° C, 375° F/ Gas 5 for about 1 hour, until the meat is tender.

Mix the grated lemon peel, parsley and remaining garlic together. This mixture, known as the *gremolata*, is a traditional component of Osso buco and serves as a piquant garnish to be sprinkled over the meat just before serving. When the veal is cooked serve on a bed of *risotto alla Milanese* (see p. 43), with the sauce poured over it and the *gremolata* sprinkled on top.

► *Osso buco*, a rich dish made from veal.

Anitra in salsa piccante (duck in a piquant sauce)

Serves 4

a $1\frac{1}{2}$-kg (3-lb) duck
2 tablespoons olive oil
50 g (2 oz) bacon, chopped
$\frac{1}{2}$ teaspoon each rosemary and sage, chopped
juice of half a lemon
salt and black pepper
100 g (4 oz) pork sausage meat
2 anchovy fillets
5 tablespoons white wine vinegar

To prepare the duck, remove the giblets (use these for a stock or soup), and wash and dry the duck and divide it into four. To do this, first

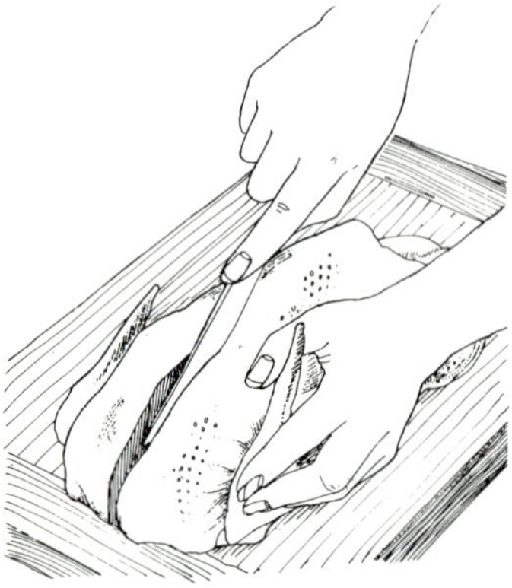

cut close to one side of the breastbone with a very sharp knife. Cut right through the breast and then through the

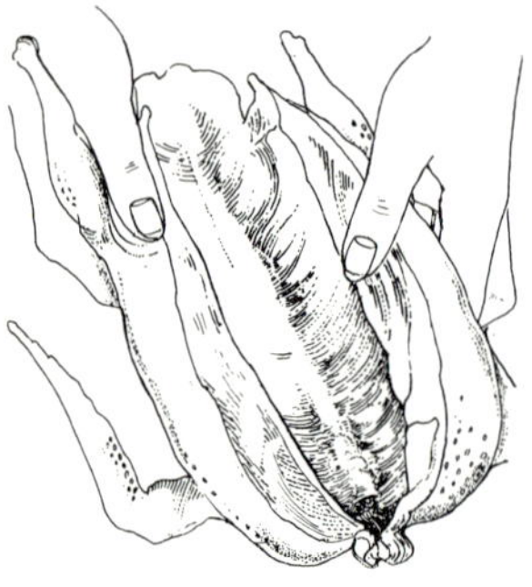

backbone, dividing the bird in half. Lay these pieces flat and with a sharp knife cut round the leg and partially

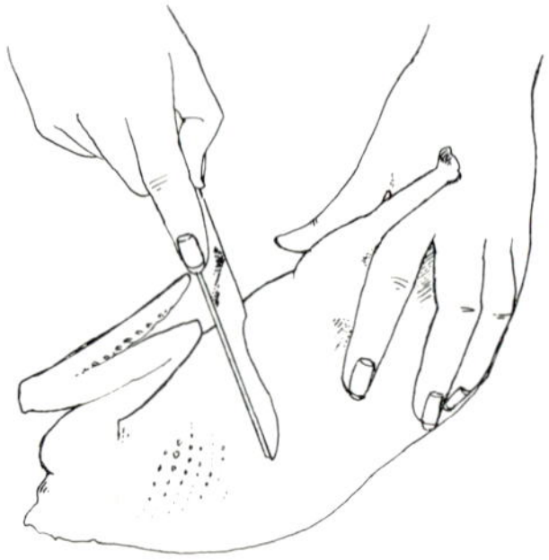

through the breast to give two reasonably equal portions from each. Then trim off the tiny end piece of the wings.

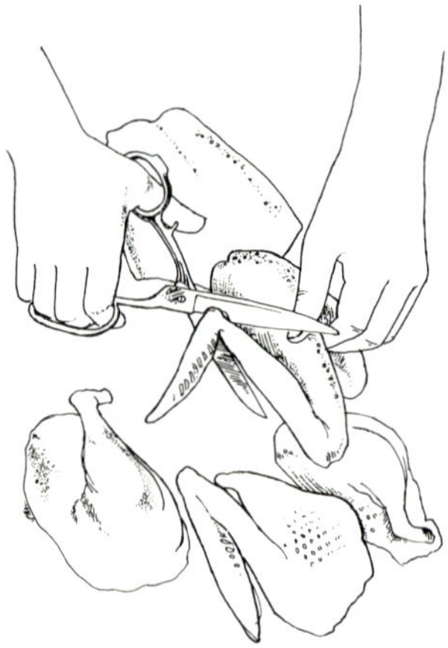

Prick all the portions, through the skin only. Melt the oil in an ovenproof dish and fry the bacon, rosemary and sage. Add the lemon juice and pieces of duck. Fry until the duck is golden on each side; then sprinkle with seasoning and place in the oven at 200° C, 400° F/Gas 6 for about 45 minutes, basting frequently. Meanwhile fry the sausage meat and anchovies gently and then add the vinegar. Stir until well blended. Drain the excess fat off the duck, cover with the sauce and continue cooking at 180° C, 350° F/Gas 4 for about 20 minutes.

Faraona alla campagnola (country-style guinea fowl)

Serves 3-4

1 guinea fowl
3 tablespoons oil
50 g (2 oz) Parma ham, chopped
25-50 g (1-2 oz) butter
1 onion, chopped
2 carrots, chopped
2 stalks celery, chopped
2 tablespoons parsley, chopped
1 teaspoon rosemary, chopped
125 ml ($\frac{1}{4}$ pint) white wine
salt and pepper

Clean, wash and dry the bird. Then brown lightly in the hot oil. Transfer to a casserole or ovenproof dish with a lid. Fry the ham, adding the butter, vegetables and herbs. After 3-4 minutes add the wine, bring to the boil and season. Pour this mixture over the guinea fowl, cover with a lid and cook at 190° C, 375° F/Gas 5 for about 40 minutes, basting frequently. When the guinea fowl is quite cooked transfer it to a serving dish and keep hot. Meanwhile sieve or liquidize the sauce, bring back to the boil and check the seasoning. Pour over the bird before serving.

Arista al peperoni (roast pork with peppers)

Serves 6

a $1\frac{1}{3}$-kg (3-lb) piece loin of pork
4-5 whole cloves
salt and black pepper
2 large or 3 small peppers
2 cloves garlic, crushed
1-2 sprigs rosemary
2 tablespoons olive oil
2 tablespoons white wine

Score the rind with a sharp knife or remove entirely if you don't like the fat. Press the cloves into the slits in the fat or the surface of the meat. Rub well with salt and place in a large roasting tin. Core and de-seed the peppers and place round the pork. Sprinkle with garlic, fresh rosemary, seasoning, oil and wine. Cover and bake at 190° C, 375° F/Gas 5 for about $1\frac{1}{2}$ hours. Remove the lid for the last 30 minutes of cooking to brown off the skin or fat if you wish. Place the pork on a serving dish, surround with peppers and drain off excess fat from the liquid before pouring a little over the peppers.

Pollo ripieno alla lucana (chicken stuffed with cheese and herbs)

Serves 4

1 small chicken
50 g (2 oz) butter
100 g (4 oz) chicken livers, chopped
salt and black pepper
2 small eggs
50 g (2 oz) Pecorino or Parmesan cheese, grated
1 tablespoon sage, chopped
1 teaspoon rosemary, chopped

Clean, wash and dry the chicken. Melt half the butter and fry the chicken livers for 2-3 minutes. Season, and beat in the eggs, cheese and herbs. When well mixed pack into the chicken, lightly sprinkled inside with salt. Then truss or fasten with a skewer. Brush the remaining fat over the chicken and sprinkle with seasoning. Roast at 190° C, 375° F/Gas 5 for about 1 hour, basting occasionally. When the juices run completely colourless from the legs of the bird, it is ready and can be served.

Scaloppe di maiale al marsala (pork fillet with Marsala)

Serves 4

675 g ($1\frac{1}{2}$ lb) pork fillet
25 g (1 oz) butter
salt and black pepper
7-8 tablespoons Marsala
1 teaspoon cornflour
37 g ($1\frac{1}{2}$ oz) butter

Trim any fat from the pork. Cut in half lengthwise and then across into small pieces. Melt the butter and fry the pork until golden. Add seasoning and the Marsala and simmer for 1 minute. Remove meat with a draining spoon and keep hot. Boil the sauce for 4-5 minutes until well reduced. Then stir in the cornflour blended with 1 tablespoon of water and cook gently until thickened. Whisk in the butter in small pieces, and when all is melted add the meat. Allow to heat through thoroughly before serving.

Stufato (beef in red wine)

This rich beef dish can be found all over Italy with many regional variations. This one comes from Lombardy.

Serves 4

900 g (2 lb) stewing or braising beef
50 g (2 oz) belly of pork, diced

Marinade:

1 carrot, diced
1 onion, sliced
1 stick celery, diced
1 clove garlic, crushed
1 bay leaf
2 cloves
250 ml ($\frac{1}{2}$ pint) red wine
grated nutmeg
salt and pepper

50 g (2 oz) butter
1 small onion, diced
6 g ($\frac{1}{4}$ oz) flour
1 bay leaf

Trim any fat off the beef and cut into large chunks. Place in a shallow bowl with the pork and the marinade ingredients. Allow to stand in a cool place overnight if possible or for at least 4 hours. Then drain the meat and pat dry. Strain the marinade, to use later.

Melt the butter and fry the chopped onion and pork until just golden and fat is beginning to run.

Sprinkle the flour over the beef to coat lightly and then fry in the fat until evenly brown. Add the bay leaf and blend in the marinade.

Cover and cook gently for about 2 hours, until meat is tender. Check occasionally that there is enough liquid in the pan; if not, top up with stock or water.

Vitello tonnato (cold veal in tuna fish mayonnaise)
Serves 6

about 1 kg (2-2¼ lb) piece of boned leg of veal
2 cloves garlic, sliced
2-3 anchovy fillets
1 small onion, chopped
2 carrots, diced
1 stick celery, diced
250 ml (½ pint) chicken stock
125 ml (¼ pint) dry white wine
seasoning
200-g (7-oz) can of tuna fish in oil
1 egg yolk
125 ml (¼ pint) lemon juice
3 tablespoons lightly whipped cream
1 tablespoon drained capers
lemon slices and black olives to garnish

Drain the tuna and set the oil aside. Make several slits in the skin of the veal and insert the slices of garlic. Place in a large pan with the fillets, onion, carrot, celery, stock, wine, seasoning and tuna. Add 125 ml (¼ pint) of water, cover, and simmer for about 1½ hours, until the meat is tender. Top up with water occasionally. Remove the meat from the pan and allow to cool. Strain the liquid, and purée or liquidize the vegetable and fish mixture with a little of the stock. Whisk the egg until pale, then gradually whisk in the oil until the sauce is thick. Continue whisking while adding the lemon juice, puréed sauce and enough stock to give a pouring consistency, (or this can be liquidized together). Season to taste, gently beat in the cream, and chill.

Slice the meat neatly and arrange on a serving dish. Mix the capers into the sauce, pour over the meat and garnish with slices of lemon and black olives before serving.

◀ From the top: *vitello tonnato; petti di pollo alla bolognese; coniglio alla molisana.*

Petti di pollo alla bolognese (breast of chicken with prosciutto and cheese)
Serves 4

4 chicken breasts
salt and black pepper
flour
50 g (2 oz) butter
5 tablespoons olive oil
8 thin slices of prosciutto (see p. 84)
8 thin slices of Bel Paese or Fontina cheese
2 tablespoons chicken stock
50 g (2 oz) button mushrooms, thinly sliced

Carefully slice the chicken horizontally to give 8 thin slices. Then flatten out as for veal escalopes (see p. 58). Season the slices lightly and then dip in flour, shaking off any excess.

Melt the butter with the oil in a large frying pan with a lid. Add the chicken pieces and cook until golden, then lay a piece of prosciutto on each one and top with a piece of cheese. Baste with hot fat and add the stock and mushrooms. Cover the pan and cook gently for 15-20 minutes, until the chicken is quite tender and the cheese has melted.

Coniglio alla molisana (rabbit and sausage on skewers)
Serves 4

a 900-g (2-lb) rabbit
salt and pepper
1 tablespoon parsley, chopped
1 teaspoon rosemary, chopped
8 small thin slices Parma ham
8 sage leaves
3-4 small Italian sausages
3-4 tablespoons olive oil

Remove the rabbit from the bone, keeping it in as large pieces as possible. Cut into 8 even pieces. Mix the seasoning with the parsley and rosemary and dip the pieces of rabbit in this. Wrap each piece in a slice of ham and arrange on skewers with the sage leaves

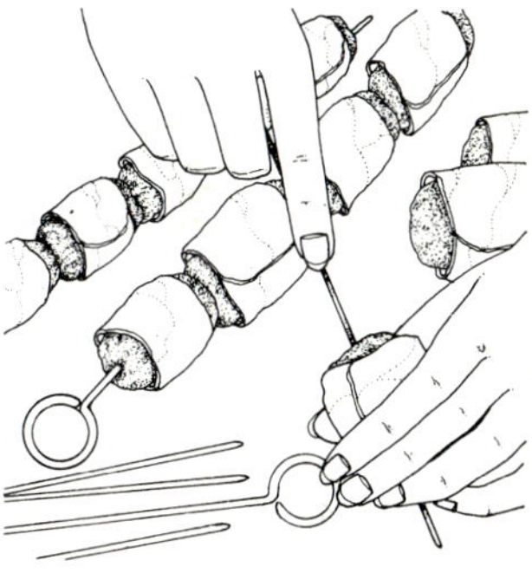

and sausages cut into small pieces. Brush well with oil and cook under a hot grill, turning and basting frequently for about 15 minutes; or bake in the oven for about 1 hour at 180° C, 350° F/Gas 4.

Saltimbocca (veal escalopes with ham and sage)

Serves 4

4 veal escalopes
4 slices Parma ham
4 sage leaves
37 g (1½ oz) butter
salt and black pepper
4-5 tablespoons dry white wine

To prepare escalopes, whether they are veal, chicken, pork or turkey, you will need 2 small sheets of greaseproof paper for every piece of meat and a meat mallet or a rolling pin.

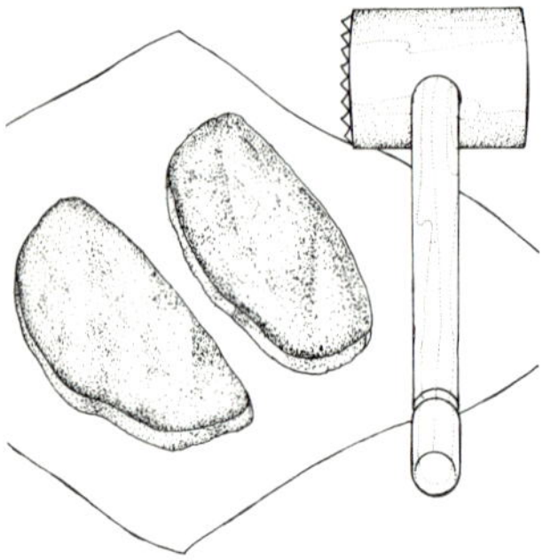

Sandwich each piece of meat between paper and with the mallet, gently flatten the meat until it is as thin as possible and about twice its original size.

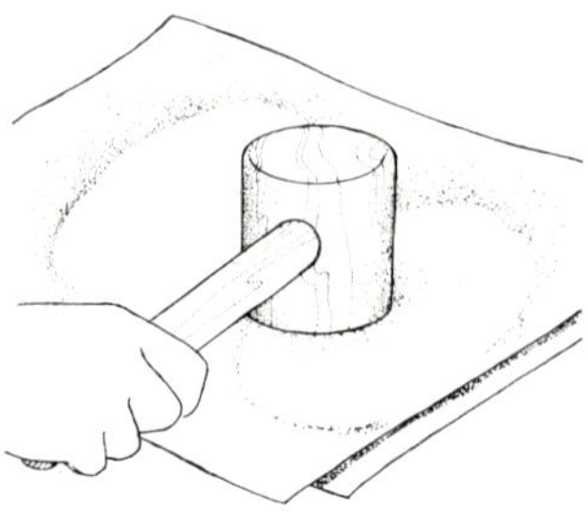

On each piece of meat place a slice of ham and a sage leaf. Secure with a cocktail stick if you wish.

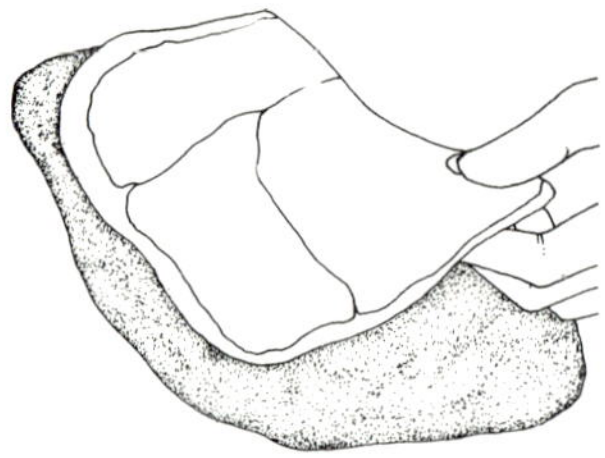

Melt the butter in a large pan and add the veal. Brown quickly on both sides, add a very little seasoning if you wish, remembering that the ham is salty. Add the wine and bring to the boil just before serving. Total cooking time should not be more

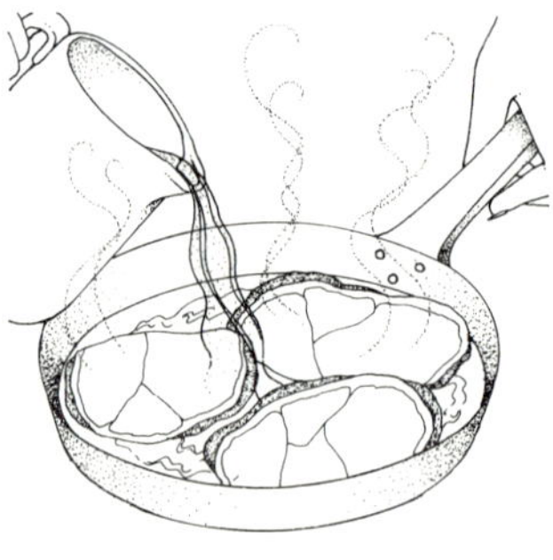

than about 5 minutes. Serve immediately with the extra sauce poured over.

If you want to thicken the sauce a little before serving, transfer the escalopes to a serving dish to keep hot. Simmer the liquid gently for about 5 minutes until reduced by half, check the seasoning and pour over the meat.

Agnello rustico (roast leg of lamb with cheese and lemon)

Serves 4

small leg of lamb
salt and pepper
4 tablespoons olive oil
1 small onion, sliced
juice of half a small lemon and 1 teaspoon rind
37 g (1½ oz) Pecorino or Parmesan cheese, grated

Season the meat lightly with the salt and pepper and set aside. Pour oil into a roasting tin with a lid, add the onion and lamb and bake at 190° C, 375° F/Gas 5 for about 35 minutes. Then spread with the lemon juice, rind and cheese mixed together and continue cooking for a further 20-30 minutes, until the meat is tender but not overcooked.

Trippa alla marchigiana (tripe with garlic, tomatoes and vegetables)

In Italy most tripe comes from veal, and is used to make many exciting dishes. However, even with ox tripe this recipe tastes very good.

Serves 4

550 g (1¼ lb) dressed tripe
salt and pepper
25 g (1 oz) butter
50 g (2 oz) bacon, chopped
1 clove garlic
1 stick celery
1 carrot
1 sprig parsley
1 small ham bone or knuckle with a little meat on it
1 teaspoon dried marjoram
1 teaspoon grated lemon rind
1 tablespoon tomato purée
half a winter cabbage
12 very small onions

Cut the tripe into 5-mm-thin strips about 5cm long. Put into a pan of cold water and bring to the boil. Season, and simmer for about 1½ hours. In another pan melt the butter and fry the bacon and vegetables until just golden. Add the parsley, ham bone, marjoram and lemon rind and the tomato purée dissolved in a little of the cooking liquid. Add the tripe and the rest of the liquid. Bring to the boil and simmer again for a further hour, topping up with extra water if necessary. Trim the cabbage and cut into 4 portions. Peel the onions and add both these vegetables to the pan about 30 minutes before cooking is completed. When the tripe is tender remove the ham bone, cutting off any meat to add to the stew. Check the seasoning before serving.

Rognoni trifolati (kidneys in Marsala)

Serves 2-3

225 g (8 oz) veal or sheep's kidneys
juice of half a lemon
25 g (1 oz) butter
2 tablespoons olive oil
1 tablespoon chopped parsley
salt and black pepper
3-4 tablespoons Marsala
1 tablespoon double cream

Skin and trim the kidneys. Drop them into a pan of boiling water with the lemon juice and leave for 1 minute. Drain, and when cool enough to handle cut into very thin slices. Melt the butter and oil and gently fry the kidneys. Sprinkle with parsley, salt and pepper. When just tender, add the Marsala and cook until reduced. Stir in the cream and serve immediately.

Coda alla vaccinara (oxtail braised with celery hearts)

Serves 4

900 g (2 lb) oxtail
salt and black pepper
a little flour
1-2 tablespoons olive oil
1 small onion, chopped
1 clove garlic, crushed
2-3 tablespoons red wine
250 ml (½ pint) beef stock
300-g (11-oz) can tomatoes
4 cloves
pinch nutmeg
1 large head celery
1 tablespoon lemon juice
1 tablespoon parsley, chopped

Cut the oxtail into small pieces, season lightly and toss in the flour. Shake off any excess flour. Heat the oil and fry the oxtail quickly until golden brown all over. Place in an ovenproof dish. Drain off any excess fat from the pan and quickly fry the onion and garlic. Stir in the wine, stock, tomatoes, cloves and nutmeg and boil for 5 minutes. Pour over the oxtail and cook, covered, for about 3 hours at 180° C, 350° F/Gas 4, topping up with water or beef stock occasionally. Meanwhile trim the celery down to the heart and cut this into small pieces. Blanch quickly in boiling water, drain and add to the oxtail about 1 hour before the end of cooking. Just before serving stir in the lemon juice and the parsley.

Fegato di vitello alla parmigiana (calf's liver with Parmesan cheese)

There are many delicious Italian recipes which use liver, of which this is one of the best. However, it is important to use calf's liver for the best result—pig's liver has a stronger, slightly more bitter taste and is not so good when just pink in the middle as the Italians would eat it.

Serves 4

450 g (1 lb) calf's liver
2 large onions, sliced
¼ teaspoon dried marjoram
¼ teaspoon dried sage
salt and pepper
4 tablespoons olive oil
3 tablespoons Parmesan, grated
2 tablespoons fine white breadcrumbs

Cut the liver into very thin slices, or ask the butcher to do it for you. Fry the onions with the herbs and seasoning in oil until golden. Then add the liver slices, a few at a time, and fry quickly until golden on the outside but still tender in the middle. When the liver is ready it should no longer be running blood. Spoon into a heatproof serving dish and sprinkle with the cheese and breadcrumbs mixed together. Place under a hot grill for about 5 minutes, until the top is golden and crisp.

This last stage can be done in the oven if you prefer but is more likely to overcook the liver. Remember—never reheat liver dishes.

Fish

The seas around Italy provide more varieties of fish than most of us might ever hope to taste. They are not only eaten in antipasti but served in an enormous range of filling main dishes.

Italy is exceptionally well off for both fish and crustaceans. Whether in the north or the south, in remote mountainous areas or large cities, you can almost always eat fish fresh from either the sea or an inland lake. The variety of fish, too, is something to be envied. Italian fish recipes are delicious, on the whole allowing the freshness of the fish to predominate rather than stifling it in many other flavours.

Some recipes call for fish lightly coated in a thin batter and quickly fried, like the *fritto misto di mare*, now popular in most countries. Much fish is salted or dried, as in previous centuries, and is still very popular, particularly as a traditional Catholic meal on Fridays.

Even with such a plentiful supply of fish there is very little waste in the local methods of cooking. All heads and bones, skins and shells are boiled up to make very good stocks used especially in fish soups. Most regions have their own fish soup speciality, but unfortunately none has gained any great renown outside Italy.

Many types of fish native to Italy are known in other countries too; but there are also many specifically regional seafood specialities, like sea truffles, sea dates and sea urchins. All are worth trying if you have the opportunity.

The Italians are also favoured with many species of fresh fish that most of us can only ever eat out of a can. Fresh tuna, for example, is a big industry in Sicily. Fresh sardines and anchovies are also abundant and taste very different from the tinned variety.

◀ *Burrida* can be made with almost as many varieties of fish as you wish – the more colourful the better.

Burrida (fish stew)

This is a Genoese dish which serves as a meal in itself and can contain almost any fish you choose, including dogfish, mullet, skate, coley, eel, squid, sardines, anchovies, prawns, tuna, gurnet, mackerel, cod and mussels.

Serves 6

900 g (2 lb) mixed fish
6 tablespoons olive oil
1 clove garlic, crushed
1 small onion, chopped
1 anchovy fillet, chopped
1 tablespoon parsley, chopped
350 g (12 oz) tomatoes, peeled and chopped
4 walnuts, ground or pounded
165 ml ($\frac{1}{3}$ pint) dry white wine
1 bay leaf
salt and black pepper
toast or fresh bread for serving

Clean all the fish and cut into small pieces. Heat the oil, and fry the garlic, onion, anchovy fillet and parsley. When softened add the tomatoes, nuts, wine, fish, bay leaf and seasoning. Bring to the boil and cook until the wine has reduced and the fish is tender. Serve immediately with the toast or fresh bread.

Lumache in zimino (snails with garlic and herbs)

Although snails are readily available canned with flavouring, in some countries they are also sold live.

Serves 4

about 6 snails per person
salt and black pepper
2 teaspoons dried mixed herbs
3-4 tablespoons olive oil
1 small onion, sliced
2 cloves garlic, crushed
sprig of fresh parsley and rosemary, chopped
100 g (4 oz) button mushrooms, finely chopped

Starve snails for about 10 days, loosely covered with a cloth in a basket. This allows all the scum to come out. Now soak the snails in salted water for about 3 hours, changing the water occasionally. Wash under cold running water until all the scum has disappeared. Then place in a fresh pan of salted water with the dried herbs. Bring to the boil, and simmer for about $1\frac{1}{2}$ hours. Strain, and remove snails from their shells, discarding the tiny black piece on the body.

Heat the oil and add the onion, garlic, parsley, rosemary, mushrooms and seasoning. Fry gently for 2-3 minutes before adding the snails. If you wish you could return the snails to their shells, cover with sauce and bake in the oven for a few minutes.

Cozze ripiene (stuffed baked mussels)

Serves 3-4

2 kg (4 pints) fresh mussels
165 ml ($\frac{1}{3}$ pint) dry white wine
salt and black pepper
350 g (12 oz) tomatoes, peeled and chopped
1 clove garlic, crushed
3 tablespoons olive oil
2 tablespoons parsley, chopped
2 tablespoons fine breadcrumbs

Put the mussels into cold water as soon as possible. Although they are best eaten the same day, if it is necessary to keep them cover the bowl with a cloth and then sprinkle with salt. Keep in a cool place. Discard any that are broken or have cracked and loose shells and any that are open.

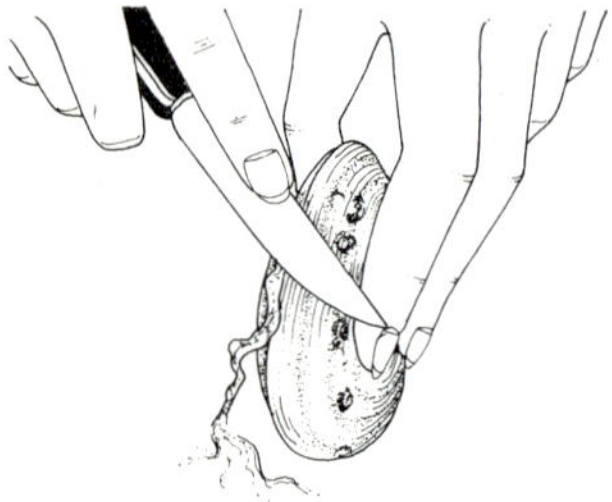

To clean them: keeping the mussels in cold water, with a sharp knife scrape away the hairy 'beard' or seaweed-like bits attached to the shell; then chip off

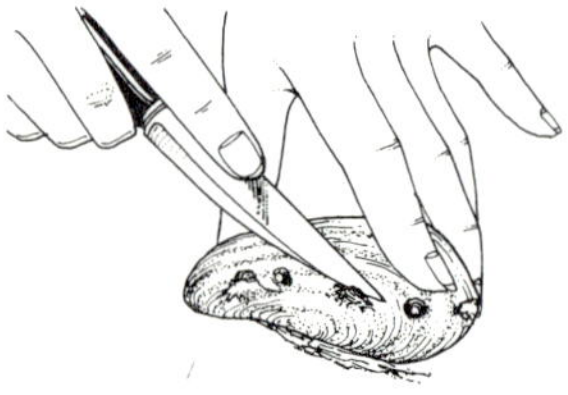

any barnacles. Finally scrub the shells thoroughly and rinse them in cold running water until there are no traces of sand or grit. Put the wine, seasoning, tomatoes, garlic and oil in a large wide pan and simmer for about 5 minutes. Add the mussels, cover, and cook gently for about 10 minutes, until they open. Discard any that don't open and transfer the rest to a large shallow ovenproof dish, removing one half of the shells. Add the parsley to the pan and simmer the tomato mixture until very soft. Spoon onto the mussels and sprinkle each one with breadcrumbs. Pour any extra wine around them and bake for about 10 minutes, or until the crumbs are brown, at 180° C, 350° F/Gas 4.

Cozze al vino bianco (mussels marinaded in white wine)

Serves 4

2-3 tablespoons olive oil
1 onion, finely chopped
1 red pepper, finely chopped
salt and black pepper
1 tablespoon parsley, chopped
juice and rind of 1 small lemon
250 ml ($\frac{1}{2}$ pint) dry white wine
2 kg (4 pints) mussels

Heat the oil in a large wide pan and gently cook the onion and pepper for 2-3 minutes. Add the remaining ingredients and the mussels cleaned as for *cozze ripiene*. Cover, and cook fast until the mussels open. Discard any that don't open and remove one half of each shell. Turn into a serving dish and chill overnight or for at least 2 hours.

Calamari alla veneziana (squid in its own ink)

The squid, otherwise known as inkfish and cuttlefish, has many relatives in Italy— octopus, totani, polipetti, and seppie for instance— which are rarely available in other countries. These creatures have only one supporting bone which is long, white and transparent. Many people are put off this dish when told how it is made but it really is very good, so it's perhaps best to avoid any explanations before tasting.

Serves 4-6

900 g (2 lb) squid, the smaller the better
2-3 tablespoons olive oil
1 small onion, chopped
2 bay leaves
salt and black pepper
125 ml ($\frac{1}{4}$ pint) dry white wine
2 tablespoons white vinegar
1 tablespoon parsley

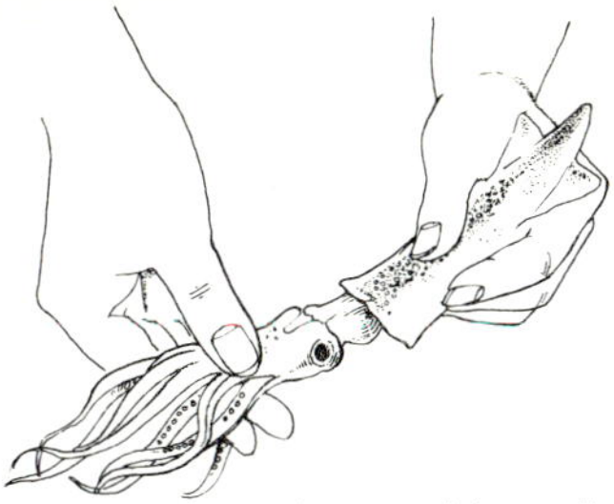

To prepare the squid, pull the head and tentacles gently out of the body. Carefully

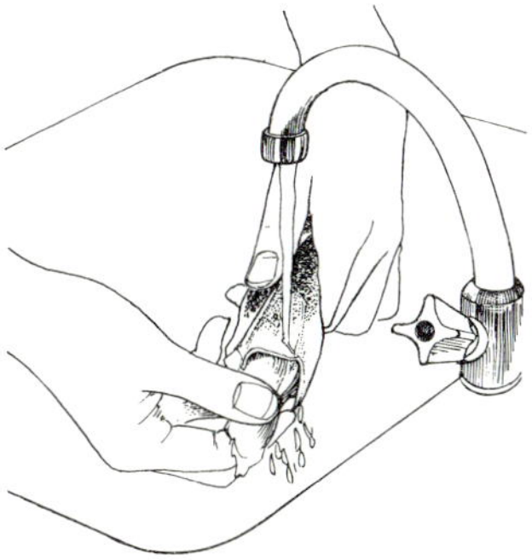

remove the ink sac (not all have one) and put in a sieve.

Wash the squid very thoroughly under cold run-

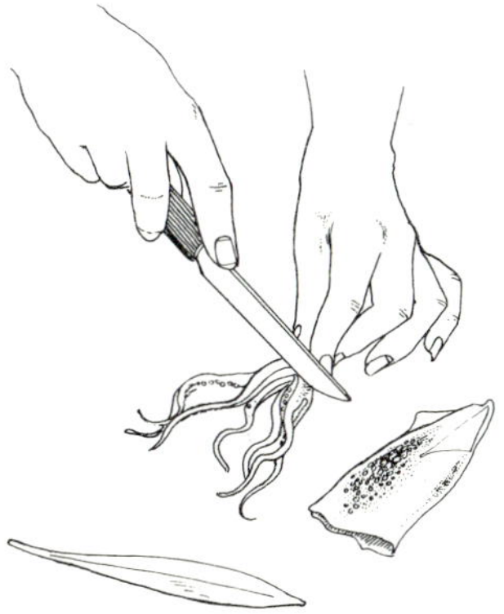

ning water, then cut away the central head part and eyes. Remove the white bony piece from the tail and fine end and peel off the outer pinkish membrane. Then cut the tentacles into small pieces and the body into 5-mm rings.

Heat the oil and fry the onion until golden. Add the fish and cook gently for 2 minutes. Then add the ink sac and other remaining ingredients and simmer, covered, for about 1 hour, until tender. Serve immediately with hot bread.

Vermicelli con vongole (noodles with clam sauce)

Serves 4

2 kg (4 pints) clams—if these are not available use mussels or cockles
olive oil
2 cloves garlic, crushed
1 tablespoon parsley, chopped
3-4 tablespoons Neapolitan tomato sauce (see p. 27)
salt and black pepper
450 g (1 lb) vermicelli

Thoroughly clean and scrub the clams as for mussels (see p. 62). Rinse well. Put 2-3 tablespoons of oil in a large frying pan and fry the garlic until golden. Add the clams, cover, and cook briskly for about 5 minutes until the shells open. Discard any that don't. Remove the clams from their shells with a sharp knife and place in a strainer. Add a little more oil to the pan, with the parsley, tomato sauce, seasoning and any liquid from the clams. Bring to the boil, add the clams and simmer for about 2 minutes. Meanwhile cook the pasta in salted boiling water as directed. When just tender, drain, and toss immediately in the sauce. This is one pasta dish where cheese is never added.

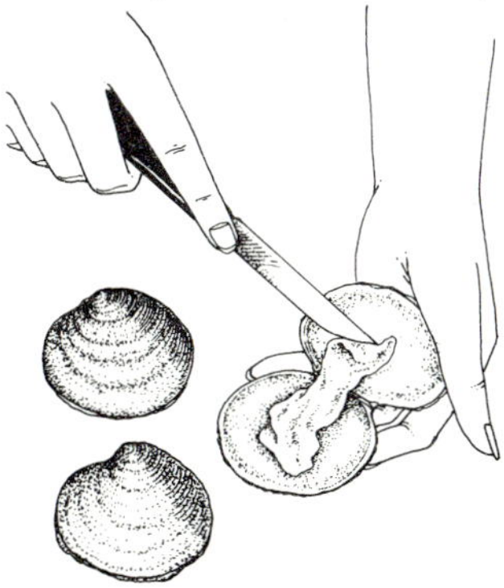

Sogliole al vino bianco (sole in white wine and raisin sauce)

Serves 4

a little oil
4 sole fillets
a little flour
2-3 shallots or 1 very small onion, sliced
salt and black pepper
165 ml ($\frac{1}{3}$ pint) dry white wine
1 bay leaf
2 tablespoons large raisins or sultanas
25 g (1 oz) pine nuts
2 cloves
1 tablespoon vinegar

Heat a little oil in a frying pan. Dip the fish fillets in flour and shake off the excess. Cook the fillets gently in the oil until golden on both sides, and transfer to an ovenproof serving dish. Keep warm. Fry the onions in the pan until golden; then add the seasoning, wine, bay leaf, raisins, nuts, cloves and vinegar. Bring to the boil, stirring, and then simmer for about 10 minutes, until the sauce has reduced. Pour over the fish and serve.

Insalata di frutti di mare (seafood salad)
Serves 4
$1\frac{1}{2}$ kg (3 pints) mussels
675 g ($1\frac{1}{2}$ lb) squid
salt and freshly ground black pepper
450 g (1 lb) shrimps or prawns
1 clove garlic, crushed
2 teaspoons French mustard
juice of 1 large lemon
1 tablespoon parsley, chopped
olive oil

Prepare the mussels as described on p. 62 and cook in a little oil until they open. Take the mussels from their shells and keep any liquid. Prepare the squid as described on p. 63, put in a large pan with the mussel liquid, salt and pepper and cook for about 2 hours, adding more liquid if necessary. Then drain the fish, shell the prawns and mix all three fish together.

Make a dressing of the garlic, mustard, lemon juice, parsley, olive oil, salt and pepper, using at least twice as much oil as lemon juice. Sprinkle over the fish, and toss before serving. Chill for 2 hours.

Scampi alla di sciullo (prawns in white wine)
Serves 4
900 g (2 lb) prawns in their shells
flour
salt and black pepper
2 eggs, lightly beaten
50 g (2 oz) butter
3 tablespoons olive oil
225 g (8 oz) mushrooms
5-6 tablespoons dry white wine
1 teaspoon parsley, chopped

Shell the prawns and devein them. Wash and dry thoroughly. Toss in seasoned flour and dip in the eggs. Heat the butter and oil together in a large pan. Add the prawns and fry gently until golden. Add the mushrooms and cook for a further minute. Then add the wine, seasoning and parsley and simmer until the wine has more or less evaporated.

Triglie alla calabrese (red mullet with black olive and caper sauce)
Serves 4
75 g (3 oz) butter
3 tablespoons olive oil
2 teaspoons dried oregano
black pepper, freshly ground
4 small red mullet or red snapper
salt
$2\frac{1}{2}$ tablespoons capers, washed and drained
$1\frac{1}{2}$ tablespoons sliced black olives
$1\frac{1}{2}$ tablespoons lemon juice
2 tablespoons parsley, chopped

Melt 25 g (1 oz) of the butter and mix with the oil, oregano, and lots of freshly ground black pepper. Heat until sizzling, in an ovenproof dish or baking tin. Then add the fish, cleaned but with head and tail still on and lightly salted inside and out. Brush the fish generously with the herb butter and then bake at 220° C, 425° F/ Gas 7 for about 25 minutes, basting frequently until crisp and the fish is just firm. Meanwhile melt the rest of the butter in a pan with the capers and black olives and heat until just turning golden. Then add the lemon juice and parsley, heat through, and pour over the fish.

Pizza calabrese (calabrian fish pie)
'Pizza' often means 'pie' in Italy, made of bread dough. This one has a fish filling.
Serves 4-6
1 quantity of pizza dough, risen (see p. 34)
50 g (2 oz) butter
olive oil
salt and pepper
675 g ($1\frac{1}{2}$ lb) tomatoes
175-g (7-oz) can tuna fish, drained
2-3 anchovy fillets, chopped
100 g (4 oz) stoned black olives, sliced

Divide the dough in two, making one piece larger than the other. Roll out the larger piece to a circle that will fit a 25-30-cm pie plate or flan dish. Fold up the edges slightly. Roll the other piece out to a round shape for the top. Leave both to rise. Meanwhile heat the butter and oil and gently cook the seasoned, peeled tomatoes until soft. Stir in the tuna, the anchovies and the olives. Place in the pie base, cover with the second piece of dough and seal the edges well with water. Brush the surface with a little melted butter or oil and bake at 190° C, 375° F/Gas 5 until risen and golden brown.

► A selection of fish dishes. Left to right: *cozze ripieni; triglie alla calabrese; insalata di frutti di mare.*

Fritto misto di mare (a deep-fried mixture of seafood)

Fritto misto can consist of either meat, any firm fish or vegetables or a mixture of all three. This seafood dish is just one of the many variations. It can include white fish such as cod, haddock, sole, plaice or coley.

Serves 4-6

675 g ($1\frac{1}{2}$ lb) squid
225 g ($\frac{1}{2}$ lb) prawns in their shells
450 g (1 lb) white fish
salt and black pepper
25 g (1 oz) flour
oil for frying
lemon segments

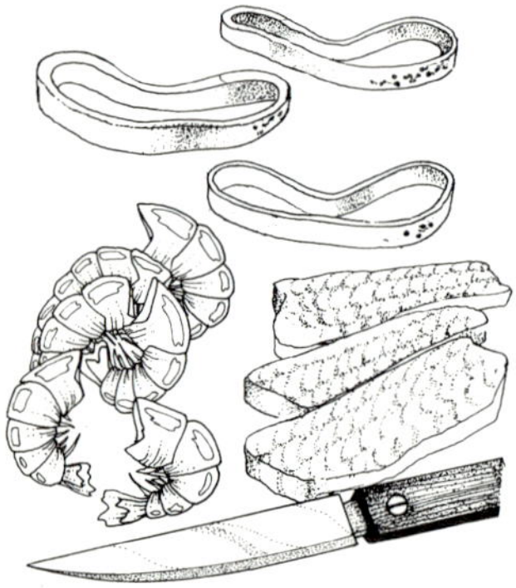

Prepare the squid as on p. 63 and then cut into rings. Place in a pan of boiling water and simmer gently for 1 hour or until tender. Drain well. Shell and de-vein the prawns, leaving their tails on.

Skin the white fish and cut into thin strips. Mix the seasoning with the flour and put on a plate. Dip the prepared fish lightly in flour and shake off any excess.

Heat a deep pan of oil until a crust of bread dropped into it turns golden in 1 minute. Put the coated fish pieces in a few at a time.

Cook for 4-5 minutes, until golden, and place on kitchen paper to drain. Continue

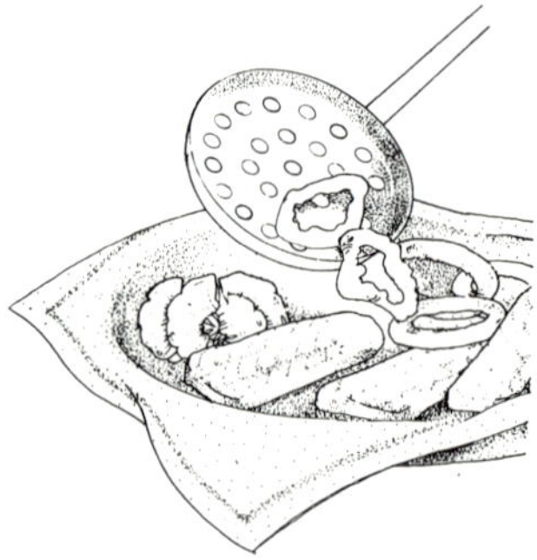

until all the fish is cooked, keeping the rest warm while you do so. Serve immediately, with lemon wedges.

Aragosta Fra' Diavolo (Lobster in wine and tomato sauce)

Serves 4

2 live lobsters 700-900 g ($1\frac{1}{2}$-2 lb) each
3-4 tablespoons olive oil
1 small onion, chopped
1 clove garlic, crushed
$\frac{1}{2}$ teaspoon lemon rind, grated
1 tablespoon parsley, chopped
$\frac{1}{2}$ teaspoon oregano or marjoram, chopped
salt and pepper
225-g (7-oz) can plum tomatoes
250 ml ($\frac{1}{2}$ pint) dry white wine

Chop off the lobster claws, and then split the body in half lengthwise. Discard the stomach (near the head), and the long intestine attached to it. Remove the greenish-brown liver and discard the small antennae under the stomach. Cut off the small claws and keep. Crack the large claws with a hammer or large knife. Carefully ease out the flesh in one piece if possible.

Heat the oil and add the remaining pieces of lobster in the shell. Cook briskly for 3-4 minutes, turning once or twice; then transfer to a warm plate, and keep warm. To the pan add the onion, garlic, lemon and herbs and fry until just golden. Then stir in the seasoning, tomatoes and wine and simmer for about 5 minutes. Return the lobster to the pan and simmer for a further 5 minutes, basting frequently. Check the seasoning just before serving.

Baccala alla vicentina (salt cod in wine and anchovy sauce)
Serves 4
675 g ($1\frac{1}{2}$ lb) salt cod cut into small pieces and soaked in cold water or milk for 24 hours
3-4 tablespoons Parmesan, grated
2-3 tablespoons olive oil
25 g (1 oz) butter
1 small onion, chopped
1 clove garlic, crushed
4 anchovy fillets, chopped
2 tablespoons parsley, chopped
125 ml ($\frac{1}{4}$ pint) dry white wine
375 ml ($\frac{3}{4}$ pint) milk

Drain the cod and place in a greased ovenproof dish. Sprinkle with the cheese. Heat the oil and butter and gently fry the onion and garlic in it. Add the anchovy and parsley and cook until softened. Add the wine and milk, bring to the boil and pour over the fish. Bake at 180° C, 350° F/Gas 4 for about 1 hour, until the fish has tenderized and absorbed much of the sauce.

Trotelle alla savoia (trout with mushrooms)
Serves 4
4 medium-sized trout
salt and black pepper
a little flour
50 g (2 oz) butter
3 tablespoons olive oil
2 shallots or 2-3 spring onion stalks, chopped
1 teaspoon lemon rind, grated
2 tablespoons parsley, chopped
225 g (8 oz) button mushrooms, sliced

Keeping the trout whole, gut and clean them well. Sprinkle inside with salt and then coat lightly in seasoned flour. Heat the butter and oil in a frying pan large enough to take all 4 trout. Gently cook the shallots, and add the lemon rind and parsley. Fry one trout at a time, turning once, until golden on each side. Add the mushrooms and return the trout to the pan. Cover and cook for a further 10 minutes, basting and turning occasionally. When just firm transfer to a serving dish and pour the sauce over.

Anguille arrosto (roast marinaded eels)
Serves 4
550 g ($1\frac{1}{4}$ lb) eels
125 ml ($\frac{1}{4}$ pint) olive oil
salt and black pepper
juice of 1 small lemon
1 small onion, sliced
8 sage leaves
4 sprigs rosemary

Cut the eels into slices about 5cm thick. There is no need to peel off the skins for this dish. Place them in a large shallow dish with the oil, seasoning, lemon juice and onion. Marinade for at least 1-2 hours. Drain well and then arrange pieces of eel alternately with onion rings on metal skewers with the sage leaves and crumbled rosemary.

Either bake in the oven or cook under a very hot grill, basting with the marinade every few minutes.

When the skin is crisp and the flesh is tender the eels are ready to serve. They can be eaten hot with the extra marinade and hot bread or allowed to cool in the marinade and served chilled.

Eel can also be fried before it is marinaded. Toss pieces in lemon juice and flour, then fry in olive oil for 4-5 minutes. Add to a hot marinade: onion, garlic, peppercorns, herbs and salt fried in oil then simmered with white wine. Leave to chill overnight.

Vermicelli con le cozze (noodles with mussels)
A recipe from Naples, where mussels are to be had in abundance.
Serves 4
1-$1\frac{1}{2}$ kg ($2\frac{1}{2}$-3 pints) mussels
olive oil
salt and pepper
3 cloves garlic, crushed
1 tablespoon chopped parsley
450 g (1 lb) vermicelli (see p. 88)

Clean the mussels as directed on p. 62. Heat 2-3 tablespoons of oil in a large pan and fry the garlic gently. Add the mussels and cook, covered, for about 5 minutes. Discard any that don't open. When cool, remove the mussels from their shells and return them to the pan. Add the seasoning and parsley and cook for another minute or so to heat through. Meanwhile cook the vermicelli as directed on p. 25 and drain. Toss immediately in the other ingredients, and serve topped with cheese if you wish. If you prefer, add 2-3 tablespoons of double cream to the sauce when reheating.

Cakes, pastries and sweetmeats

The Italians eat a vast number of little cakes, pastries and other sweetmeats, often bought from street stalls. We can thank them for creating, among other things, the macaroon, or *amaretti,* and the famous sticky white nougat, or *torrone.*

Cenci alla fiorentina (carnival pastry knots)

Makes about 24

100 g (4 oz) plain flour
1 small egg and 1 egg yolk, beaten together
icing sugar
salt
2 teaspoons rum
oil for frying

Sieve the flour into a large bowl. Add the egg, 2 or 3 teaspoons of sugar and a pinch of salt. Knead well, gradually adding the rum until the mixture is smooth but pliable. Cover with a damp cloth and leave for about 20 minutes. Then divide the dough in two and roll out each piece separately on a floured board until wafer thin. Cut into 10-cm-long and 1-cm-wide strips and tie into knots. Heat the oil. Drop in the pieces of dough a few at a time and cook for about 2 minutes, until golden brown and crisp. Drain on kitchen paper while cooking the rest. Sprinkle well with icing sugar before serving. Eat as soon as possible.

Torta di noci (ground nut cake)

Serves 8-10

350 g (12 oz) mixed nuts ground together
a little butter and flour
4 eggs
225 g (8 oz) granulated sugar
rind of 1 lemon, grated
a few flaked almonds
icing sugar

Have the nuts ready before you start. Grease a 20-cm cake tin and line with greaseproof paper. Separate the eggs and beat the yolks and sugar together until pale and thickened. Beat the whites until stiff. Gently and evenly fold in the lemon rind, the egg whites and the ground nuts. Pour into the prepared tin, sprinkle with almonds and bake at 180° C, 375° F/ Gas 5 for about 1 hour, or until the top is golden and the cake just firm to the touch. Cool slightly, turn out on a wire rack and leave to cool further. Sprinkle lightly with icing sugar before serving.

◀ Clockwise from the top: *cassata alla siciliana; torta di noci;* Florentines; *cenci alla fiorentina.*

Ricole (tiny spiced doughnuts)

Serves about 4

37 g ($1\frac{1}{2}$ oz) sultanas
4-5 tablespoons Marsala or sweet sherry
12 g ($\frac{1}{2}$ oz) fresh yeast or 6 g ($\frac{1}{4}$ oz) dried
25 g (1 oz) castor sugar
225 g (8 oz) plain flour
pinch salt
few drops vanilla
rind of 1 lemon, grated
$\frac{1}{4}$ teaspoon ground cinnamon
50 g (2 oz) candied peel
oil for frying
icing sugar

Soak the sultanas in the Marsala until plump and swollen. Blend the yeast with 1-2 tablespoons warm water and a pinch of sugar and set aside until frothy. Sieve the flour into a bowl with the sugar, salt and vanilla essence. Add the yeast gradually with the lemon rind, cinnamon, peel and sultanas in their liquid. Add 1-2 tablespoons more water if necessary to give a soft consistency. Cover and leave in a warm place for about an hour, until doubled in size. Then turn onto a floured surface and knead until the dough is firm again. Drop small balls of this dough into a pan of hot fat and cook, a few at a time, for about 3 minutes, until puffed up and golden. Drain on kitchen paper and serve, dredged with icing sugar.

Maringa all'italiana (Italian meringue)

This is a cooked meringue mixture which is perfect for decorating gâteaux, desserts or ices. It also makes individual meringues.

2 egg whites
150 g (5 oz) castor sugar
a drop of vanilla essence

Whisk the egg whites until stiff. Meanwhile dissolve the sugar in 1 tablespoon of water and then boil rapidly until you have a thick but clear syrup. Gradually pour this onto the whisked egg whites beating all the time until the mixture is very smooth and shiny and firmly holds its shape. Cool, and use as required. This mixture will stand well for an hour or so if covered lightly. To use as a covering for a cake, blend in the ground nuts or a little flavouring to complement the flavour of the cake. This mixture also makes cakes and desserts lighter and sweeter.

Cassata alla siciliana (Sicilian cake with cream cheese and chocolate)

Serves 10

1 large sponge cake, either round, oblong or square, or 2 thick sponges
450 g (1 lb) Ricotta, or the same quantity of good cottage cheese plus 2 tablespoons double cream
50 g (2 oz) bitter chocolate
2-3 tablespoons castor sugar
2-3 tablespoons Grand Marnier
1 teaspoon lemon rind, grated
50 g (2 oz) chopped candied peel
25 g (1 oz) chopped shelled pistachio nuts

Chocolate coating:

225 g (8 oz) bitter chocolate
2 tablespoons fresh orange juice
3-4 tablespoons milk
175 g (6 oz) unsalted butter

Cut the sponge cake into as many thin layers as possible. Press the cheese through a sieve and, if using cottage cheese, add the cream. Roughly chop the chocolate into small pieces.

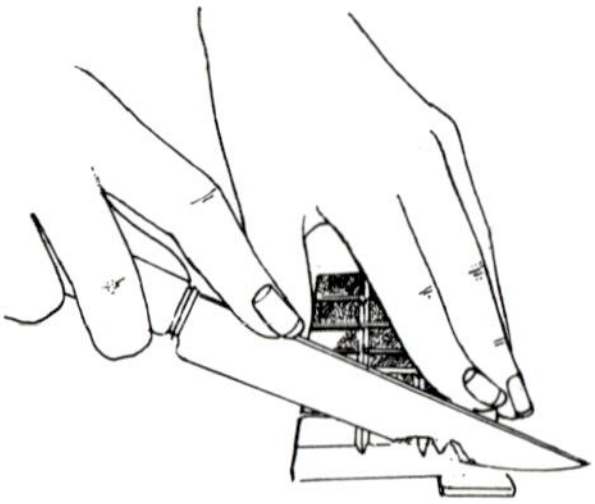

Add the chocolate to the cheese as well as the sugar, liqueur, rind, peel, nuts and chocolate. Mix well together.

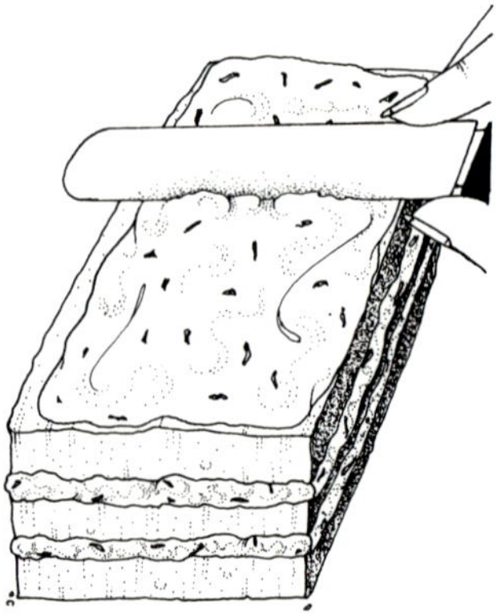

Spread all but one slice of sponge with a layer of cheese mixture and layer up. Top with the remaining slice. Chill well at this stage until firm.

Meanwhile melt the chocolate in a pan over hot water with the orange juice and the milk, without stirring. When the chocolate is soft stir gently to blend, then remove from the heat. Gradually stir in the butter in small pieces, beating until the mixture is creamy. Chill until it is a spreading consistency.

With a palette knife, spread this mixture smoothly and evenly all over the top and sides of the cake. Make a decoration on the sides if you wish with the knife or a fork. Use the remaining mixture to pipe a decoration on the top.

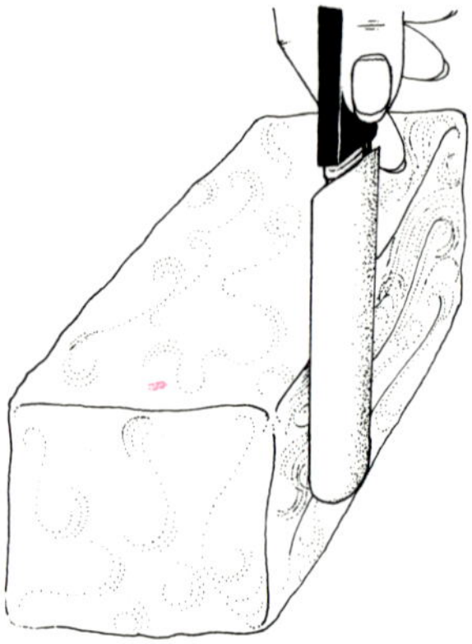

Place a large star nozzle in a large piping bag and fill with the remaining mixture. Squeeze all gently

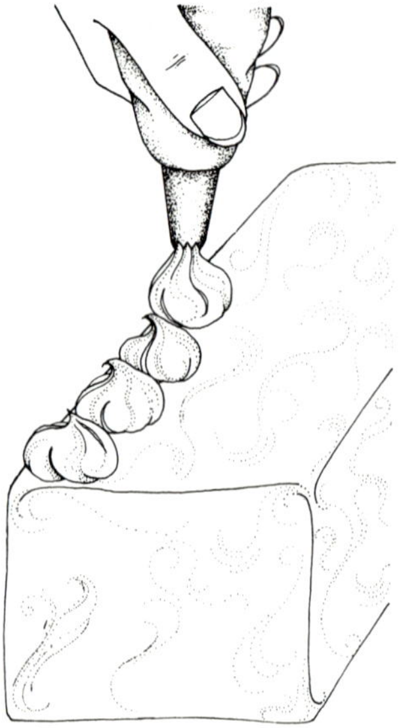

down to the nozzle end to get rid of any air bubbles. Twist the top firmly and hold the bag at the top with one hand. Use the other hand to guide the nozzle while the top hand gently squeezes the mixture down the tube. Refrigerate the cake for several hours to let the flavours mingle before serving.

Crostata alla crema (custard tart)

Serves 6

Pastry:
- 225 g (8 oz) plain flour
- 100 g (4 oz) butter
- 75 g (3 oz) castor sugar
- 2 egg yolks
- pinch salt
- rind of 1 lemon, grated

Custard:
- 2 eggs
- 75 g (3 oz) castor sugar
- 500 ml (1 pint) milk
- 1 level tablespoon cornflour
- 2 tablespoons double cream
- rind of 1 orange, grated

a little butter and flour
2 tablespoons milk or beaten egg for glaze
icing sugar

Sieve the flour into a bowl and rub in the butter until it resembles fine breadcrumbs. Gently stir in the egg yolks, salt and lemon rind and knead until the mixture comes clean from the side of the bowl. Chill for a few minutes. To make the custard blend the eggs and sugar together until creamy. Blend a little of the milk with the cornflour and heat the rest of the milk until almost boiling. Stir in the cornflour mixture until thickened and smooth. Then blend in the eggs, cream and orange rind. Return to the pan and cook gently for a further 2-3 minutes.

Roll out the pastry and grease and flour a 20-cm pie plate or dish. Line the dish with pastry and pour in the custard mixture. Decorate the top with any extra pastry and glaze with egg or milk. Bake at 190° C, 375° F/Gas 5 for about 30 minutes, until just firm and golden. Cool, and sprinkle lightly with icing sugar.

Florentines

Makes about 18

50 g (2 oz) butter
75 g (3 oz) castor sugar
2 tablespoons whipped cream
100 g (4 oz) slivered almonds
- 2 tablespoons flour
- 2 tablespoons candied peel
- 2 tablespoons chopped glacé cherries

For the coating:
- 100 g (4 oz) bitter chocolate

Melt the butter and sugar gently and when dissolved add the cream. Stir well and let it boil for a minute. Thoroughly mix in the almonds, flour, peel and cherries, and drop small spoonfuls of this mixture, placed well apart, onto greased baking sheets. Bake at 180°C, 350°F/Gas 4 for about 10 minutes, until golden brown. Cool, and place on a wire rack. Meanwhile gently melt the chocolate in a bowl over hot water. Spread one side of the cooled biscuits with the chocolate and draw wavy lines down it with a fork. Leave the biscuits until they are quite cold.

Torrone di Cremona (Italian nougat with nuts and honey)

Makes about 550 g (1½ lb)

450 g (1 lb) toasted whole almonds
225 g (8 oz) granulated sugar
1 teaspoon lemon rind, grated
pinch cinnamon and nutmeg
7-8 tablespoons clear honey
2 egg whites, whisked

Chop the almonds finely and mix with the sugar, rind and spices. Warm the honey, then stir in the nut mixture and heat gently until all the sugar has dissolved. Boil until the mixture turns golden. Remove from the heat and very quickly fold in the stiffly beaten egg whites. Pour into a shallow tin 20-cm square and lined with rice paper. Allow to cool slightly before cutting into squares.

Tartufi di cioccolata (chocolate truffles)

Makes about 12

100 g (4 oz) bitter chocolate
37 g (1½ oz) butter
1 tablespoon milk
1 egg yolk
25 g (1 oz) cocoa

Melt the chocolate and gradually blend in the butter, milk and egg yolk. Chill, and form into shapes. Coat in cocoa powder. Eat within 2 days.

Panettone (fruit bread)

A very light fruit bread which Italians often eat for breakfast and, traditionally, at Christmas and Easter.

Serves 10-12

25 g (1 oz) fresh yeast or 12 g ($\frac{1}{2}$ oz) dried yeast
4 tablespoons warmed milk
100 g (4 oz) soft butter
3 tablespoons sugar
3 eggs
350 g (12 oz) plain flour
pinch salt
3 tablespoons raisins
2 tablespoons candied peel
2 tablespoons milk or beaten egg for glaze

Cream the yeast with the milk and leave until frothy, about 10 minutes. Cream

the butter and sugar together until light. Then beat in the eggs. Sieve the flour and salt into a large bowl and gradually mix in the

yeast liquid and the egg mixture. Mix until you have a soft but kneadable dough, adding extra milk if necessary.

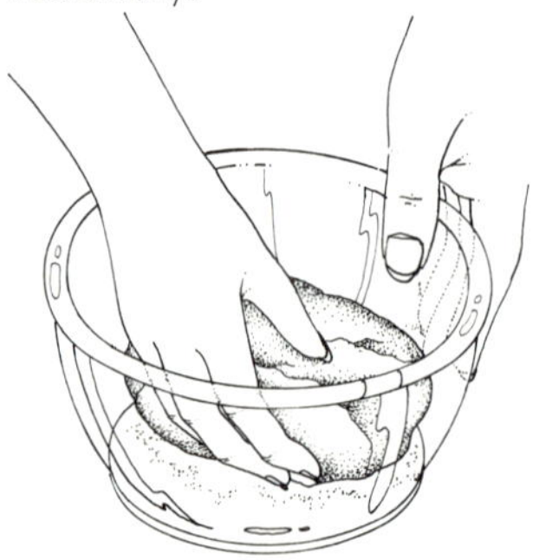

Turn out onto a floured surface and knead until smooth. Place in a floured

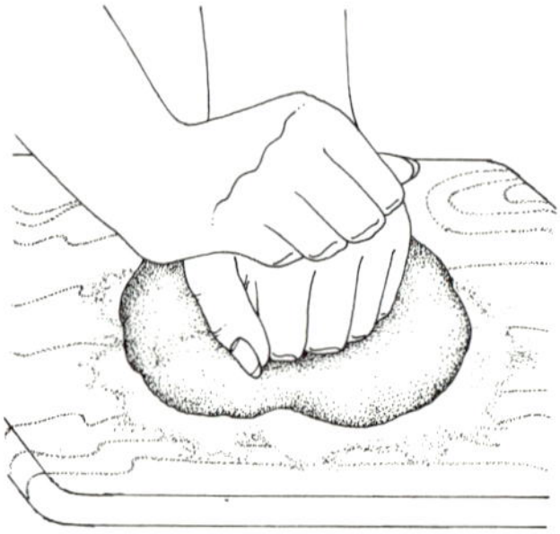

bowl and cover. Leave in a warm place to double for about 1 hour. Then turn out

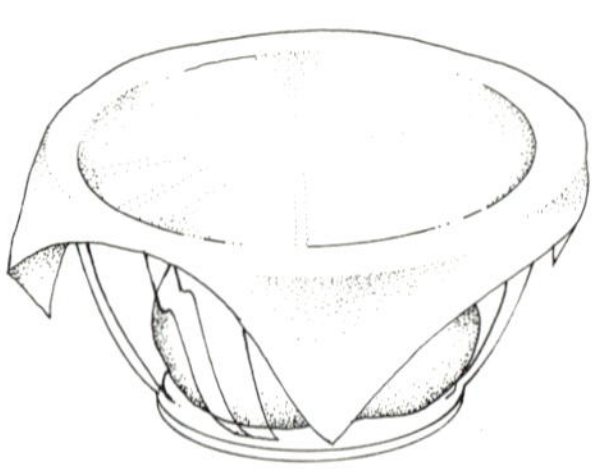

onto a floured surface again and flatten. Sprinkle the fruit and peel over, fold over and flatten to encompass the fruit. Then knead gently until firm again.

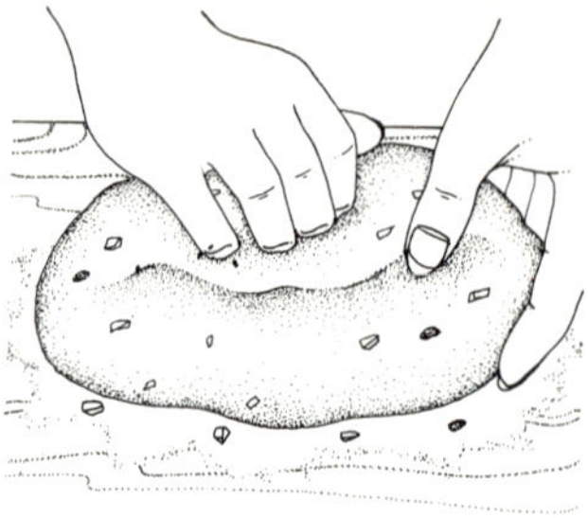

Form the mixture into a ball and place in a 20-cm greased cake tin. Cover and leave in a warm place again until doubled in size once more. Glaze the top with egg or milk and bake at 200°C, 400°F/Gas 6 for 10 minutes. Then reduce the heat to 180°C, 350°F/Gas 4 for a further 30 minutes or until the mixture is well risen, golden and firm to the touch. Cool on a wire rack. Keep the panettone well wrapped to aid storage.

Budino di panettone (panettone pudding)

This is a popular way of using up panettone, or any other light sweet bread. Soak 6 slices in 3-4 tablespoons of rum and Marsala. Bring 250 ml ($\frac{1}{2}$ pint) milk to the boil with 1 piece of lemon rind and $\frac{1}{4}$ teaspoon of cinnamon flavouring; then cool. Beat 2 egg yolks and sugar to taste into the milk and then stir in the slices of cake. Whisk 2 egg whites until stiff and fold into the mixture. Spoon into a greased pudding basin and bake in a *bain-marie* for about 1$\frac{1}{2}$ hours. Allow to cool and then turn out before serving.

▶ *Crostata di ricotta.*

Cheesecakes

For many people this word now conjures up a vision of something totally removed from the simple, homely cheese pudding that the Italians often eat as a light dessert.

Not many people realize that cheesecake recipes have been around for thousands of years. In recent years the cheesecake has arrived on every restaurant menu, on every supermarket shelf and in almost every home. It has become the fashionable dessert to serve all over Europe; but in Italy it has long been a popular everyday pudding.

The Romans first created cheesecake using a cheese somewhat like the Ricotta we know today. Many versions are called Roman cheesecake, but no two recipes are the same. Many other versions are called 'Ricotta pudding'—for this is what the early cheesecake recipe really was. Ricotta cheese (one substitute is cottage cheese, although it is not as good) is mixed with eggs and a variety of fruits, or crumbs and then baked. It can be flavoured with many things; encased or just topped; and served hot or cold. Here are some old and some new versions.

Crostata di ricotta (Roman cheesecake)

Serves 6-8

Pastry:

225 g (8 oz) plain flour
175 g (6 oz) soft butter
4 small egg yolks
2 tablespoons castor sugar
2 tablespoons dry Marsala or sherry
½ teaspoon lemon rind, grated
pinch of salt

Filling:

900 g (2 lb) Ricotta or curd (or cottage cheese, with 3 teaspoons double cream)
100 g (4 oz) castor sugar
3 tablespoons flour
pinch of salt
a few drops of vanilla essence
4 egg yolks
2 tablespoons sultanas
2 tablespoons candied peel
egg white for glaze
2 tablespoons slivered almonds

Sieve the flour into a bowl and add the butter, yolks, sugar, Marsala, lemon rind and salt. Work gently with a fork to bring all the ingredients together. Then knead lightly only until all is smooth. Wrap in foil and chill. Meanwhile prepare the filling.

Mix the cheese with the cream and sieve into a bowl. Add the sugar, flour, salt, vanilla and yolks and beat until thoroughly blended. Then mix in the sultanas and peel.

Roll out the pastry on a lightly floured surface. Try not to add too much flour; but if you do find it is too sticky, roll out between two sheets of greaseproof paper. It should be a circular shape large enough to line a loose-bottomed 20-cm flan ring and leave a little over for decoration. Gently fold the pastry over the rolling pin to ease placing it in the tin. Mould into the corners of the tin to give well-shaped sides. Trim off the excess and cut into long thin strips. Bake the pastry case blind, for about 15 minutes at 350°F, 180°C/Gas 4.

Fill the pastry case with the cheese mixture, arrange the extra pieces of pastry in a lattice on top and glaze with egg white. Sprinkle with almonds and bake at 180°C, 350°F/Gas 4 for about 1 hour, until the crust is golden and the filling is just firm. Remove from the oven and allow to cool slightly. Then stand the dish on a large jam jar or coffee tin to enable the loose sides of the tin to slide down.

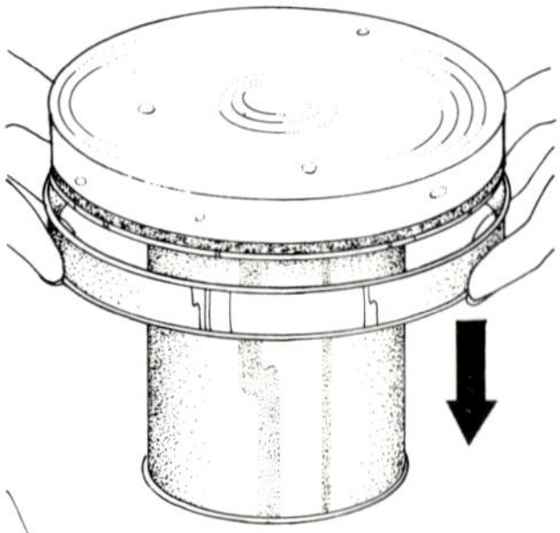

With two fish slices or palette knives lift the cheesecake off the metal base and onto a serving dish. It will be easier to do this while the cake is slightly warm. Leave until cold before serving.

Budino di ricotta (ricotta cheese pudding)
Serves 6
25 g (1 oz) sultanas
25 g (1 oz) raisins
2 tablespoons rum
250 g (10 oz) Ricotta
4 egg yolks
100 g (4 oz) castor sugar
50 g (2 oz) ground almonds
1 tablespoon flour
pinch of cinnamon
rind of 1 small lemon, grated
vanilla essence
4 egg whites

Soak the sultanas and raisins in the rum until swollen. Sieve the cheese and beat in the egg yolks, sugar, almonds, flour, cinnamon, lemon rind, a few drops of vanilla, the fruits and the rum. Beat well. Whisk the egg whites and fold in. Pour into a greased basin or dish and bake at 190°C, 375°F/Gas 5 for about 1 hour. You can either serve this hot or allow to cool before turning out and serving cold.

This is perhaps the most elaborate version of Ricotta pudding. You can omit the almonds, the rum or the dried fruit if you wish. There is also a Sicilian version where the filling is cooked between two layers of pastry, more like a pie.

Cheesecake

This international variation of the basic cheesecake recipe is more like a very light sponge with a creamy texture and a slight cheesy tang.
Serves 6-8
6 eggs
350 g (12 oz) castor sugar
125 ml ($\frac{1}{4}$ pint) sour cream
250 ml ($\frac{1}{2}$ pint) double cream
37 g ($1\frac{1}{2}$ oz) flour
675 g ($1\frac{1}{2}$ lb) cream cheese
grated rind and juice of half a lemon
75 g (3 oz) flaked almonds

Grease and line a 20-cm cake tin, preferably one with a loose bottom. Separate the eggs and beat the yolks with the sugar, cream and the flour until smooth and well blended. Beat the cream cheese until really soft, and beat in the lemon juice and rind. Gradually beat in the egg mixture, but do not over-beat. Whisk the egg whites until stiff, and fold carefully into the cheese mixture with the almonds. Blend well but without knocking out all the air, then spoon into the tin and bake at 170°C, 325°F/Gas 3 for about $1\frac{1}{2}$ hours. The cake should be golden on top but will still feel quite soft to the touch. Allow to cool well before turning out of its tin. Chill well before serving.

Orange cheesecake

This is our more modern version of the cheesecake which is not cooked but set with gelatine.
Serves 6-8
150 g (6 oz) shortcrust pastry
675 g ($1\frac{1}{2}$ lb) cream cheese
225 g (8 oz) castor sugar
a few drops vanilla essence
juice and rind of 1 large orange
25 g (1 oz) gelatine
250 ml ($\frac{1}{2}$ pint) whipped cream
4 egg whites, stiffly beaten
25 g (1 oz) toasted almonds
1 orange, sliced

Roll out the pastry to a circular shape 20cm in diameter and line the base of a loose-bottomed cake tin with it. Prick the pastry well and bake at 190° C, 375° F/Gas 5 for about 20 minutes, until crisp. Cool well.

Beat the cream cheese until softened and beat in the sugar, essence, orange juice and rind. Dissolve the gelatine in 2 tablespoons of hot water and when completely clear blend into the cheese. Fold in the whipped cream and the egg whites. Spoon over the pastry into the greased tin and chill for at least 1 hour. Turn out as on p. 74, decorate the sides with the remaining orange slices and sprinkle the almonds on top.

The cheese mixture can be varied by the addition of other fruits such as pineapple, strawberries or cherries, either in the mixture or used on top of the filling to make a decorative layer. Add spices like nutmeg and cinnamon, or add coconut, crushed biscuits or nuts to give more texture.

► Overleaf: a selection of ice creams and water ices, or *granite*. Left to right: vanilla; coffee granita; orange granita; peach; *tortone;* lemon and lime granita; pistachio; strawberry granita; peach; chocolate and walnut; vanilla.

Ices

Genuine Italian ice cream is becoming a rarity nowadays even in Italy: there as elsewhere the mass-produced variety is taking over. No manufacturer, however, has ever been able to capture the truly delicious flavour of the real thing.

Gelato (ice cream)

Good ice cream is expensive so it is worth making well. If you don't have an ice-cream-making machine don't let this worry you – you just need time and patience. Don't stint by adding less expensive flavourings.

Makes about 1 litre (2 pints)

375 ml ($\frac{3}{4}$ pint) single cream
small piece vanilla pod or a few drops essence
100 g (4 oz) castor sugar
8 egg yolks
375 ml ($\frac{3}{4}$ pint) double cream

Gently heat the single cream and vanilla pod in a large pan to scalding point. (If you are using vanilla essence, reserve until later.) Meanwhile whisk the sugar and yolks together until thickened and very pale. Remove the vanilla pod, pour the hot cream onto the eggs, whisking all the time, and then return to the pan. Again heat gently, in the top of a double saucepan if possible, until the mixture thickens to the consistency of thin custard. You will need to stir most of the time to prevent thickening on the bottom and sides. Now pour in the double cream, and the essence if you are not using a vanilla pod. Strain, and leave to cool. Then pour into your ice-cream machine, or into ice trays and place in the freezer. Without a machine you will need to take the ice cream out and beat once or twice at least every half hour for about 2 hours, until very stiff. Then beat more thoroughly before returning to freeze solid.

Remember when making ice cream to turn the freezer to the coldest possible temperature. It can take up to 3 or 4 hours to freeze. Whenever possible allow the ice cream to soften for a couple of minutes before serving.

Gelato cioccolata e noci (chocolate and walnut ice)

Follow the previous recipe exactly, but when adding the double cream beat in 100 g (4 oz) of melted plain chocolate and then stir in 50 g (2 oz) of finely chopped walnuts. These may make it difficult to use a blender, but will make no difference when beating by hand.

Gelato pistacchio (pistachio ice)

Use the previous recipe, less the walnuts, chocolate and 2-3 tablespoons of sugar. Add $1\frac{1}{2}$ tablespoons of ground or crushed shelled pistachio nuts while cooking the custard. Then stir in the double cream and a few drops of green food colouring. Strain, then add $4\frac{1}{2}$ tablespoons chopped shelled pistachio nuts, and 3 tablespoons of ground almonds. Cool, and freeze as before.

Gelato pesca (peach ice cream)

When making fruit ice creams use only half of the original quantities for vanilla and then when cool stir in a fruit purée made from 225 g (8 oz) of fresh or 150 g (6 oz) of dried peaches, apricots or other firm fruit. Simmer the chopped fruit with water until very soft, and sieve. If it seems to be too watery simmer for a few minutes longer to evaporate. Allow the fruit to cool before blending it into the custard.

For strawberry and other soft-fruit mixtures add the pulp from 675 g ($1\frac{1}{2}$ lb) of fruit. This can simply be puréed if the fruit is very soft, or simmered with no sugar until tender. Remember to sieve well to get rid of the tiny seeds.

Granita (flavoured water-ice)

Makes about 750 ml ($1\frac{1}{2}$ pints)

Orange:

375 ml ($\frac{3}{4}$ pint) water
150 g (6 oz) sugar
375 ml ($\frac{3}{4}$ pint) orange juice
juice of 1 lemon

Dissolve the sugar in the water and bring to the boil. Cook the syrup for about 5 minutes, until it is thickening but still clear. Stir in the orange and lemon juice and pour into a freezing tray. Freeze, stirring every 30 minutes with a fine whisk until the texture is fine and snowy. If preferred, freeze in the ice-cube section of the refrigerator until solid; then turn out and crush.

Raspberry or strawberry:
Make a syrup as above, but with only 100 g (4 oz) sugar. Then stir in 250 g (10 oz) fresh fruit, puréed or sieved, and $1\frac{1}{2}$ tablespoons of lemon juice.

Coffee:
Omit the orange and lemon juice and stir in 375 ml ($\frac{3}{4}$ pint) brewed coffee.

Lemon and lime:
Make the syrup with 50-75 g (2-3 oz) more sugar than for orange water-ice. In place of the orange and lemon juice, stir in 185 ml ($\frac{3}{8}$ pint) lemon and lime juice mixed.

Tortoni (ice cream made with macaroons)

This ice takes its name from the man who created it in the seventeenth century in Paris, where it became an instant success.

Serves 8

2 egg whites, softly beaten
500 ml (1 pint) double cream
6 tablespoons icing sugar
200-225 g (7-8 oz) crushed macaroons
1 tablespoon rum
1 tablespoon toasted almonds

Beat the egg whites until stiff, gradually adding the icing sugar until the mixture is stiff. Mix together half the cream with the macaroons and rum. Beat the rest of the cream until stiff. Fold in the macaroons and whipped egg whites and spoon into a freezer tray or basin. The mixture can also be frozen in individual portions. Serve topped with the flaked toasted almonds.

Cassata gelata

These are flavoured ices frozen in a pudding basin, and sometimes made to look like a cake. This is a time-consuming dish to make, but worth the effort. A cassata basin will be useful if you intend to use it every day. Otherwise, it is not really worth the cost, and a pudding basin and plenty of ice cubes will suffice.

Serves 6-8

$\frac{1}{3}$ quantity chocolate ice cream as given on p. 78
$\frac{1}{3}$ quantity peach ice as given on p. 78
250 ml ($\frac{1}{2}$ pint) whipping cream or double cream
1 teaspoon sugar, or to taste
$2\frac{1}{2}$ tablespoons candied fruits, finely chopped
$2\frac{1}{2}$ tablespoons almonds, chopped

Have the first two ices ready made, and a $1\frac{1}{4}$-$1\frac{1}{2}$-litre ($2\frac{1}{2}$-3-pint) pudding basin in the freezer chilling well. Coat the basin with a thick layer of chocolate ice, packing it well into the bottom of the basin to give a good shape. Return to the freezer until firm. Then pack in a thick layer of the peach ice in just the same way and freeze again. If the ice cream softens at this stage, place the basin in a large bowl filled with ice cubes, to keep the temperature down.

Finally whip the cream, adding a little sugar, and then fold in the fruits and almonds. Fill the empty space with this mixture, tap gently to make sure all the cracks are filled up and return to the freezer for another 2-3 hours.

To turn out, dip the basin into hot water for a few seconds, place a wetted plate on top and then invert,

shaking firmly at the same time to loosen.

Quick ice cream

Ice cream must be made with the best ingredients; it also calls for a lot of time and patience. Here is a recipe that is quicker than the conventional one and, when enriched with fresh cream, ideal for using up a glut of fruit.

Makes about 675 ml ($1\frac{1}{2}$ pints)

1 can of custard, or 500 ml (1 pint) custard
250 ml ($\frac{1}{2}$ pint) whipped cream
250 ml ($\frac{1}{2}$ pint) fruit purée

Fold the custard, cream and fruit purée gently together and spoon into an ice tray. Allow to freeze for a short time before stirring. Give a good stir every 30 minutes for about 2 hours, until frozen. Cover and seal for long-term storage.

Desserts

The Italians, like much of the rest of the world, are getting more conscious of their weight and their health in general. They may still eat large platefuls of pasta, but the traditional elaborate gâteaux are rapidly disappearing, especially from restaurant menus.

Zabaione (whipped Marsala custard)

Allow these quantities per person:

2 egg yolks
2 teaspoons sugar, or to taste
1 small sherry glass of Marsala (sweet sherry or sweet white wine may be substituted)

Put the egg yolks, sugar and Marsala in a large bowl over a pan of simmering water. Make sure it is a large bowl as the mixture will expand a lot during cooking. Whisk with either a hand or electric whisk over the hot water until the mixture becomes very pale and fluffy and

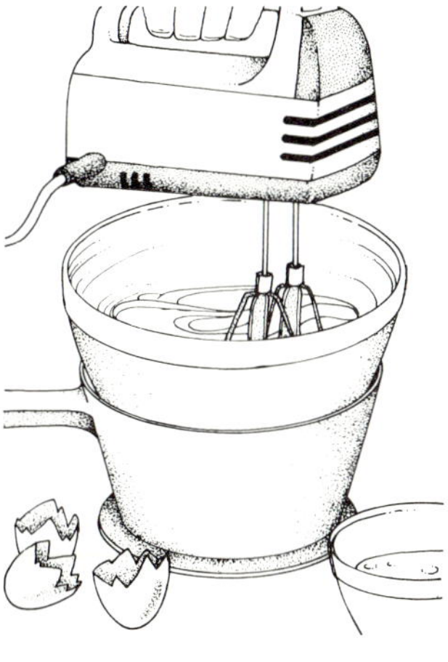

leaves a trail in the bowl when you lift up the whisk. Be careful not to boil or overheat this mixture as it will curdle. It may take about 10-15 minutes of careful watching. As soon as it is ready pour into warmed glasses and serve with little sweet biscuits, macaroons or ratafias.

The Italians sometimes make this dessert with Sambucca—an Italian liqueur. Follow the recipe above, replacing the Marsala with Sambucca and increasing the sugar to taste.

◀ A glass of *zabaione* served with sweet biscuits.

Busecchina (chestnuts stewed in white wine)

Although this should be made with dried chestnuts, it is just as good made with fresh chestnuts, when they are available.

Serves 4

350 g (12 oz) shelled chestnuts
165 ml ($\frac{1}{3}$ pint) dry white wine
2 tablespoons sugar
juice and rind of half a lemon
165 ml ($\frac{1}{3}$ pint) cream

Soak the chestnuts overnight in the wine. The following day simmer them gently in the wine with the sugar and the lemon rind and juice, until most of the liquid has evaporated. Serve chilled with the cream poured over.

If you particularly like chestnuts, prepare several times the recipe when chestnuts are in season, then bottle them and keep for 2 to 3 months before using.

Fighi al cioccolato (figs in chocolate sauce)

Serves 3-4

350 g (12 oz) good dried figs
50 g (2 oz) ground almonds
50 g (2 oz) candied peel
25 g (1 oz) chopped walnuts
cinnamon
75 g (3 oz) bitter chocolate

Remove any stalks from the figs and make a pocket in the middle of each with a small sharp knife. Mix together the almonds, peel, walnuts and about $\frac{1}{4}$ teaspoon of cinnamon. Press a little of this mixture inside each fig and press the fig back into shape. Place on a baking sheet and bake at 180° C, 350° F/Gas 4 for about 15 minutes, until darkened. Meanwhile melt the chocolate and blend in 2 tablespoons of hot water. Coat the figs in this when they are ready and either allow to cool, coated in chocolate, or serve hot in the chocolate sauce.

Crema al mascarpone (cream cheese with sugar and rum)

Mascarpone is an unsalted creamy cheese made mainly in Lombardy. It is like home-made cream cheese and often served plain with fruit, or lightly salted for other uses.

Serves 4-6

225 g (8 oz) Mascarpone, or other unsalted cream cheese or clotted cream
50 g (2 oz) sugar
2 eggs, separated
2-3 tablespoons rum
pinch cinnamon

Beat together the cheese, sugar and egg yolks. Then carefully blend in the rum and cinnamon. Whisk the egg whites until stiff and fold in. Spoon into individual dishes and serve chilled.

Pesche ripiene al gorgonzola
(peaches stuffed with Gorgonzola)

This may sound like a very strange combination, but the result is a very pleasant creamy mixture of flavours.

Serves 4

4 fresh peaches, or 8 canned halves, drained
$2\frac{1}{2}$ tablespoons lemon juice
50 g (2 oz) Gorgonzola
25 g (1 oz) softened butter
2 tablespoons walnuts, crushed
sour cream

Peel and stone the fresh peaches or dry the canned ones thoroughly. Cream the lemon juice, Gorgonzola, butter, and walnuts together thoroughly. Spoon the mixture into the peach halves; chill; and serve with sour cream poured over.

Aranci caramellati
(caramelized oranges)

In Italy this is made with Sicilian oranges, which have no pips. However, it makes little difference which you use – it still tastes very good.

Serves 4

4 oranges
175 g (6 oz) sugar
1-2 tablespoons brandy or Kirsch for extra flavour (optional)

Cut the tops and bottoms off the oranges so they stand completely flat. Always try to prepare oranges for this dish on a plate or over a bowl to catch any juice dripping. With the orange upright, carefully slice between the skin and the flesh with a sharp knife, removing all the white pith but taking

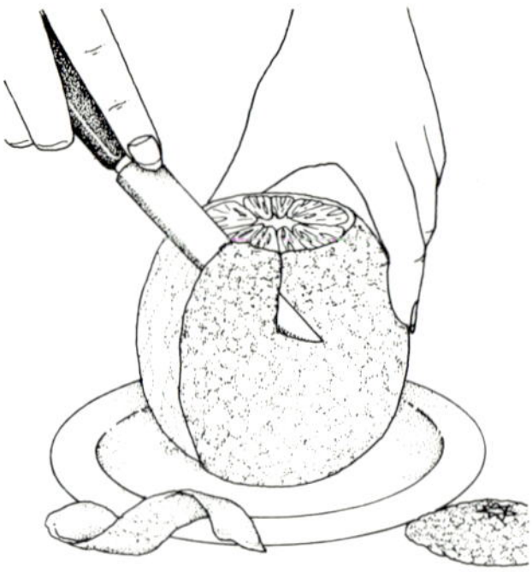

away as little flesh as possible. Reserve the peel. This way you can end up with a nicely rounded orange when peeled. Now cut into the natural segments being careful to avoid the dividing skin. Meanwhile dissolve the

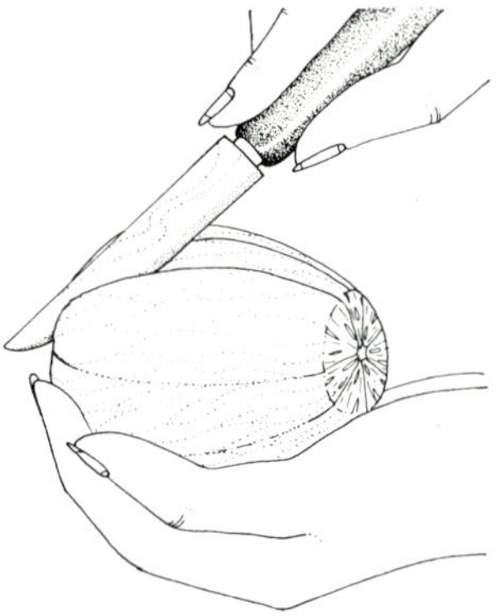

sugar in 3 tablespoons of water and when really clear boil until this turns to a light golden caramel. Remove from the heat immediately and allow to cool slightly. Remove the white pith from the peel and cut the peel into long thin shreds. Add the oranges and peel to the syrup. Cool, stirring occasionally, and serve well chilled. Double cream is the ideal accompaniment to this dish. Arrange the orange segments attractively as you serve them.

Monte Bianco Maria Luisa
(chestnut purée with cream)

Serves 4

350 g (12 oz) chestnuts, fresh peeled, or canned
500 ml (1 pint) milk
vanilla pod or a little vanilla essence
100 g (4 oz) sugar
2 tablespoons unsalted butter
1 tablespoon Cognac
165 ml ($\frac{1}{3}$ pint) double cream, whipped
2 teaspoons icing sugar

Place the chestnuts in a pan with plenty of cold water and bring to the boil. Cook for 10 minutes. If using canned chestnuts drain them well. Then place the chestnuts in another pan with the milk and vanilla and simmer until tender. Meanwhile dissolve the sugar in a pan in 2 tablespoons of water and boil until syrupy. Drain the chestnuts, and sieve. Mix with the syrup, butter and Cognac and mix to a very smooth paste. Using a piping bag or spoon, place neatly onto serving dishes, leaving a space in the centre of the dish about the size of an apple. Chill the chestnut purée, and mix together the whipped cream and icing sugar. Serve with the whipped cream spooned into the middle of each dish.

Italian cheeses and meats

CHEESES

Italy produces probably the most widely varied selection of cheeses of any country in the world. Many Italian cheeses are renowned throughout the world for their quality and most of the ones shown here should be fairly easy to find.

Parmigiano Reggiano, or Parmesan cheese, has until recent years been known as 'Grana', from its closely grained texture. It is this, and the shade of its pale yellow colour that show the cheese's quality. It takes two years to mature.

Parmesan is the perfect grating and seasoning cheese for pasta dishes, as it never goes stringy. It should be freshly grated just before using. Stored in the 'fridge tightly wrapped it will keep for months.

Pecorino is a hard cheese made from goats milk. In many parts of Italy and in many foreign restaurants it is often served instead of Parmesan. It too has to be well matured and is a very good grating cheese. It is often eaten on its own by the Italians. There are many versions of this cheese throughout Italy, the best known being **Pecorino Romano** and **Pecorino Sardo** from Sardinia.

Fontina is a very popular cheese from the Piedmont region. It is creamy, with a high fat content, and occasionally has tiny holes, in common with Gruyère. It melts well for use in sauces and **fonduta.**

Provolone is a delicate creamy cheese when fresh, with a soft but firm texture. After two to three months the flavour sharpens. It is good eaten fresh but is also suitable for sauces. Provolone is made in many different shapes and sizes.

Caciocavallo is similar to Provolone. It was originally so called because the cheeses when strung together in pairs look as if placed astride a horse.

Dolcelatte is a new Italian cheese which has become popular only in very recent years. It is made from Gorgonzola blended with a cream cheese, producing a soft yet sharp cheese that is delicious to eat on its own. It should be bought as and when required, since it ripens quickly.

Mozzarella is a cheese from buffalo or cow's milk. This very pale creamy-white cheese has a very slight sour tang. It is pleasant either eaten fresh or as an ingredient of a huge range of cooked dishes. Although readily available in most places now as a smoked cheese with a yellow rind, the very best fresh moist Mozzarella is hard to come by. It is best kept in water, to hold in the moisture.

Taleggio is a well-flavoured soft creamy cheese which becomes runny on ripening.

Bel Paese is a very mild creamy cheese for those with not such hardened palates. It is good for cooking as well as being a popular table cheese.

Gorgonzola is the only blue-veined Italian cheese. It is made from cow's milk and, although originally allowed to grow mould naturally, nowadays this process is often speeded up by the use of copper wires. It is a creamy, sharp cheese too good to be cooked.

Ricotta is a very white, soft cheese made from unsalted milk, not unlike cottage cheese but creamier. It is good for many cooked dishes but is locally eaten with sugar and fruits.

SALAME AND CURED MEATS

Well known throughout the world are Parma ham, Mortadella and salame—but that is only the beginning of Italy's range of speciality meats. Each region makes its own sausages, salames, cured meats and other local favourites to old and well-tried recipes. Few of these foods are exported to other regions, let alone to other countries. The following list includes several that are readily available outside Italy; but many you will still only be able to buy in good delicatessens or shops in London (see p. 91).

Prosciutto di Parma is the speciality of Parma in Emilia-Romagna. The hams, after salting, are hung for half a year to dry. The town of Langhirano is widely held to have the best air for curing hams, and every year large quantities of hams from other parts of Italy are sent there to be aged. No modern techniques can help in the curing process sufficiently to reduce the cost of this delicacy.

Salame

Despite some industrialization, the individuality of local salame recipes is still respected, and they are followed with great care. The difference of each salame is dependent on the kinds of meat used, the proportion of fat to meat, and the methods of chopping, mixing, seasoning and curing.

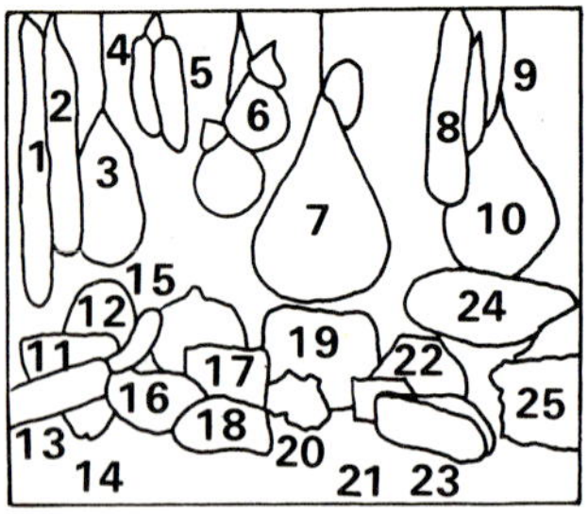

SOME ITALIAN CHEESES AND MEATS

1 Felino salame
2 Genovese salame
3 Coppa di Parma
4 and **15** Cacciatori
5 and **16** Provolone
6 Caciocavallo
7 Prosciutto di Parma
8 Milano salame
9 Cotechino
10 Mortadella
11 Fontina
12 Zampone
13 Bresaola
14 Pig's trotter
17 Parmigiano Reggiano
18 Dolcelatte
19 Taleggio
20 Mozzarella
21 Gorgonzola
22 Ricotta
23 Bel Paese
24 Prosciutto cotto
25 Pecorino

FORMAGGIO MOLLE DA TAVOLA
TALEGGIO
galbani
GALBANI
Mozzarella
SALAMI
Negroni
MORTADELLA

Milano salame is the most readily available. It has a fine texture and is seasoned with pepper, garlic and white wine.

Felino salame, although difficult to find, has a much purer meat flavour because of its very high pork content. It is spiced with peppercorns.

Fiorentina and Varzi salame are made from much coarser mixtures of pork and fat.

Cacciatori are small salames, similar to the Milan salame.

Sardinia produces its own salame, **Sardo,** which is flavoured with red pepper.

Cotechino is a large pork salame which undergoes a longer curing process than other salames. It needs to be simmered for a few hours, before being eaten hot.

Zampone is a similar mixture to Cotechino but is stuffed into the skin of a pig's trotter. This meat, too, has to be cooked.

Mortadella is not cured, like the salames, but very gently steam-cooked. The best variety is made from pure pork, but veal and other meats are sometimes introduced. It is often flavoured with whole black peppercorns, or pistachio nuts. The very smooth pink texture is thought to have been originated in the monasteries, where a process of pounding the pork in a mortar was formerly used.

Bresaola is very different from the meats given above. It comes from a particular cut of beef which is smoke-cured to produce very dark red, moist meat. It has a very delicate, slightly sweet flavour and is cut paper thin, like Parma ham.

The wines of Italy

Although Italy produces a great many wines, very few travel well. Those that do, fortunately include some of the very best, which are exported in vast quantities. But you may still find limited supplies of an Italian wine whose quality and value for money not everyone has come to recognize. Listed below are some of the most famous Italian wines.

Reading the label

Understanding Italian wine labels can be difficult as they have little uniformity of meaning. Wines can be named after a village, region or even the grape. Some producers print the region of production – but they don't have to. The most reliable mark on any Italian label is 'D.O.C.': Denominazione di Origine Controllata. This describes any defined and controlled area producing specific wines approved by the Italian Wine Committee. These wines are subject to certain controls and testing and must wear the D.O.C. label. The very best-quality wines are also entitled to carry a gold and black government seal around the neck of the bottle.

Some code words

amabile or *abbocato*	medium sweet
amaro	very dry
casa vinicola	the wine firm
classico	from the best part of the region
consorzio	growers' association with legal standing
dolce	very sweet
frizzante	half sparkling – it just tingles on your tongue
imbottigliato	estate bottled
riserva	better quality
secco	dry
spumante	sparkling
vendemmia	vintage

NORTH-WEST ITALY

Piedmont is the heart of the wine production of north-west Italy, producing some of the best mature wines.

Barolo is one of the greatest and most famous Italian wines. It is a smooth, full bodied red wine with a strong scent. It is best at about three years, and quite rough when too young. It should be stored upright, not on its side, as it has a sediment.

Barbaresco is a near relation to Barolo. Although full bodied it is slightly drier. Both these wines are good accompaniments to the rich foods of the region.

Barbera is a dark red wine. It has a sharp, acidic taste but qualifies as good though slightly rough.

Asti In contrast this region also produces the well-known Asti Spumante, a sweet and sometimes sticky sparkling white wine.

NORTH-EAST ITALY

The wines of this region, particularly around Verona, are harder and less pungent than those from Piedmont even though the grape is often the same.

Soave is probably the most famous from this region. It is a delicate, dry, very pale white wine. It has a distinctive bouquet and flavour and is at its best when it is young. Look for

Soave Classico, which is more expensive perhaps, but better.

Lambrusco This is an unusually exciting wine, for although it is red it is also **frizzante** – just a little sparkling. It is good with rich foods but also goes well, when chilled, with sweet dishes.

Valpolicella is a dark cherry colour, and has a sweet smell and a soft light flavour with just a hint of bitterness when you swallow. It will go well with most dishes, since it is strong enough for highly seasoned foods and yet will not overpower delicate flavours.

Bardolino is a very light red wine, almost rosé. It is less substantial than Valpolicella, and is slightly dry with a pleasantly bitter flavour, like almonds, which is common to many red wines of this region.

CENTRAL ITALY

Here is the home of Chianti, perhaps the best-known of all the Italian wine. But the region also produces many good white wines.

Chianti was the first Italian wine to adopt the D.O.C. system, having already used a similar system. There are still many Chiantis produced in adjoining areas, often with very similar labels. Many are extremely good: for instance, Chianti Rufina. Chianti Classico is the category of wines to look for: in particular, Chianti Brolio. The best Chiantis, well aged in the oak before bottling, appear in a Bordeaux-shaped bottle. This, in particular, distinguishes them from the many other Chiantis, which have a varying characteristic shape of flask in a straw case. Wines in this type of flask are meant to be drunk young.

Orvieto was traditionally a fragrant sweet white wine, incidentally the favourite of many popes in the Middle Ages. Now a pleasantly dry and fruity Orvieto is also produced, and is sometimes in bulbous straw flasks.

Frascati is a favourite Roman table wine. It is straw-coloured, with a somewhat unexpected taste, for although it has a sweet flavour of ripe fruit it really is dry.

Verdicchio dei Castelli di Jesi is a delightful all-purpose wine from the Marches of Central Italy. This is a pale, dry white wine full of flavour but not too heavy, and very good with fish dishes. It is easily recognizable by its unusual green sharply waisted bottle.

SOUTHERN ITALY

Few wines from this region are well known elsewhere.

Lacrima Christi is perhaps the best known. Nowadays this is more of a brand name than anything more specific, used of red and white wines from around Naples. Although generally of reasonable quality they can be disappointing.

▼ Some characteristic bottle shapes. Left to right: Verdicchio, Frascati, Soave, Chianti, Valpolicella, Barolo.

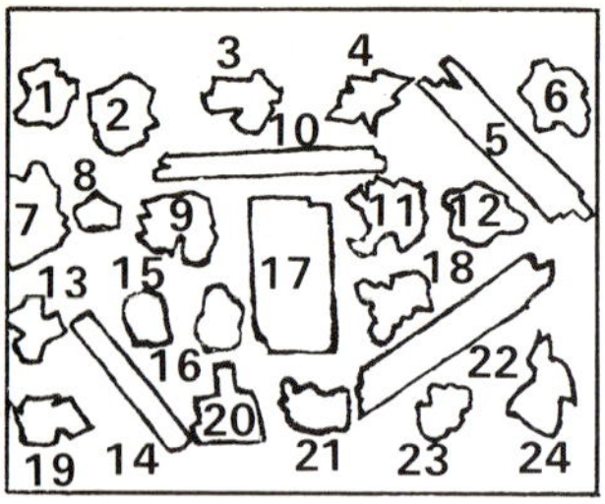

Pasta checklist

1 *Tortellini*—tiny 'little hats', to be filled with meat or cheese, cooked and served with a sauce.
2, **6**, **7** and **12** are all *tagliatelle*, also known as *fettuccine*. **2** is wholemeal; **6** is *tagliatelle verdi*; **7** is dried, egg-enriched; **12** is freshly made.
3 *Grosso rigata*, usually cooked and then stuffed.
4 *Pennini*.
5 *Zitoni*, long macaroni—can be broken up or left whole.
8 *Anellini*—tiny soup shapes.
9 *Tortiglioni*—spirals.
10, **14** and **22** are three different thickness of spaghetti: *capellini*, *spaghettini* and *spaghetti*.
11 *Farfalle*—'bows'.
13 *Ravioli*—little cushions of pasta filled with meat or cheese. Can be bought freshly cooked.
15 *Stelline*—soup pastas.
16 *Conchigliette*—soup pastas.
17 *Lasagne verdi*, used layered for lasagne, or filled and then rolled, for cannelloni.
18 *Conchiglie*—'shells'.
19 *Granigna rigata*.
20 *Cannelloni*—cook, then stuff with a meat or cheese filling and serve with a sauce.
23 *Nocchette*—a soup pasta.
24 *Penne*.

Metrication

All the recipes in this book have been given in both Imperial and metric measurements. It is important that you use one or the other and do not mix them.

To convert both solid measure and liquid measure to metric it is more convenient to use units of 25. The true conversions are very difficult to measure on most equipment.

Solid measure

1 oz	25 g
2 oz	50 g
4 oz	100 g
8 oz	225 g
16 oz (1 lb)	450 g
2 lb	900 g

1 kg (1,000 g)	just over 2 lb
½ kg (500 g)	just over 1 lb

Liquid measure

1 fl. oz	25 ml
¼ pt (5 fl. oz)	125 ml
½ pt	250 ml
¾ pt	375 ml
1 pt	500 ml

Oven temperatures

Gas Mark	°F	°C
¼	225	110
½	250	130
1	275	140
2	300	150
3	325	170
4	350	180
5	375	190
6	400	200
7	425	220
8	450	230
9	475	240

Book list

Although there are many very good Italian cookery books in addition to the titles mentioned below, there are also many very interesting European and international cookery books which include an Italian section and are well worth looking at.

Italian Food, Elizabeth David, Penguin, 1977, 90p. The hardback version of this book, published many years ago was so popular that now a paperback version is available. Written in her own delightfully chatty and knowledgeable style, it gives much background information and methods of cooking. It includes helpful hints about Italian ingredients and very many really good recipes.

The Home Book of Italian Cookery, Beryl Gould-Marks, Faber and Faber Ltd, 1969, 95p. A good, concise collection of descriptions of the regions and their specialities.

Portrait of Pasta, Anna del Conte, Paddington Press Ltd, 1976, £3.95. An amusing historical look at pasta through the ages with many delightful black and white pictures and prints, and anecdotes about the people who made various pasta recipes famous. The second half of the book deals purely with the cooking of pasta and its many recipes.

Italian Regional Cooking, Ada Boni, Thomas Nelson & Sons Ltd, 1969, £4.50. This book contains a very thorough look at the different regions of Italy, their history, the foods of each region and many traditional local recipes. Several large colour pictures show off the terrain, the tourist spots and much delicious food.

The Cooking of Italy, Time Life Books, consultant editor Margaret Costa (part of the Time-Life Foods of the World series, only available by subscription to Time-Life International). A very comprehensive and well-illustrated book, explaining much about the history of Italian food, with delightful stories describing the local cuisine, and many step-by-step colour pictures.

The Pasta Cook Book, Myra Street, Hamlyn, 1974, £1.50. An easy-to-follow collection of good Italian recipes with a selection of enticing colour pictures.

Italian Family Cooking, Mary Reynolds, Hamlyn, 1979, £3.95. A good collection of recipes that all the family can enjoy, with many superb colour pictures and much regional information.

Pasta, Pasta, Ursel Norman, William Collins, 1975, £1.50. A paperback delightfully illustrated with fun colour drawings of many of the recipes. Describes economical but good home cooking.

A Taste of Rome, Theodora Fitzgibbon, J. M. Dent & Sons Ltd, 1975, £4.50. Includes historical black and white prints of places and people linked with classic and famed Italian dishes. It gives a very good insight to the Rome of not so long ago. Good reading, with delicious recipes.

Italian Desserts and Pastries, Leone Bosi, Lutterworth Press, 1974, £3.95. Probably the only book that deals purely with the sweet side of Italian food. Again historically illustrated, it contains many simple, and several more complicated, dishes.

The Recipes That Made a Million: Food for the Famous, Franco Lagattolla, Orbis, 1978, £4.50. Written by one of the partners in the Mario and Franco London chain of restaurants, it includes many of the recipes favoured in their restaurants by famous people. Although this book provides very good reading, its cooking is not for beginners.

MAGAZINES

Although there are no British magazines that specialize in Italian food, several do publish an occasional feature on it: in particular the various monthly or bi-monthly partwork series. However, there are two more specialized Italian glossy magazines that you should be able to obtain in Britain if you have a good newsagent near by. Because ot transportation costs the price is usually high – about £1.50 – but they often contain beautiful food pictures and exciting ideas for recipes. The names to look for are *Brava* and *Grazia*.

LEAFLETS

The Italian State Tourist Department of Information Office,
201 Regent Street, London W1
01-439 2311
Although this organization does not specialize in food or wine information, it can supply many leaflets and booklets about the country, which may be helpful.

Courses

There are no British cookery schools that specialize in Italian food, as there are for French food, unfortunately. However, there are many evening classes that do short courses in European cooking or in dinner-party cooking. These include many famous Italian dishes. For details of forthcoming curricula phone or write to your local education authority or Citizens' Advice Bureau.

The Pasta Information Centre,
Richmond Towers,
26 Fitzroy Square,
London W1
01-387 2639
This bureau has information on the production of pasta, its history, how to cook it and where to buy. They have five leaflets available: on general information, nutrition, general recipes, one-pan cooking and pasta parties. They will also try to answer any query you may have.

FILMS

The Pasta Information Centre also has a 20-minute colour film entitled *Adventure with Pasta*. It can be made available to schools, colleges, educational centres and other groups, and gives a very interesting account of the history and production of pasta both here and abroad.

Suppliers

Many Italian food products are now available throughout the country, especially most shapes of pasta and a selection of meats and cheeses. If you have difficulty in obtaining a particular product in your area, go to the nearest large department store with a good Food or Delicatessen Hall.

For more specialized foods you may have to search around all the small Italian delicatessens in the area. Outside London few places supply more than a rather limited selection of Italian foods. In London try the following:

Lina Stores Ltd,
18 Brewer Street,
London W1
01-437 6482

Fratelli Camisa,
1a Berwick Street,
London W1
01-437 7120

Parmigiani Figlio Ltd,
43 Frith Street,
London W1
01-437 4728

Angelo Salvo,
19 Sussex Street,
London SW1

Vinorio No. 8,
8 Old Compton Street,
London SW1
01-437 1024

Harrods,
Knightsbridge,
London SW1
01-730 1234

Selfridges,
Oxford Street,
London W1
01-629 1234

Glossary

Al dente: literally translated, this means 'to the tooth'. Pasta should be cooked just to this degree – still slightly firm in the middle.
Baccala: dried salt cod; very popular not only in Italy but also in Spain and Portugal.
Bain-marie: a large shallow dish or tin used containing a 2-5-cm depth of water. Used for cooking delicate foods at a constant minimum temperature, with the container of food sitting in the water.
Baking blind: to bake pastry cases without a filling. The raw pastry case is lined with foil or greaseproof paper and filled with dried beans or bread crusts during baking to prevent the sides of the pastry falling.
Béchamel sauce: a white sauce made with milk that has been previously flavoured with onion, carrot, spices and herbs.
Blanching: putting foods into boiling water for a very short time: **(1)** to remove skins from nuts, tomatoes etc.; **(2)** to kill enzymes before freezing the food and to seal in the colour and flavour; **(3)** to remove very strong or bitter flavours.
Bouquet garni: a bunch of herbs and spices, usually parsley, thyme, a bay leaf, marjoram, cloves and peppercorns, tied together, and used to flavour savoury dishes. It can be bought in a small muslin bag, and should be removed from the food before serving.
Calamari: a species of small squid.
Cassata: an ice-cream dish made with two or three layers of ice cream inside a pudding basin. Usually it has two or three different flavours and often a fruity centre.
Cotechino: a type of highly spiced pork sausage.
Cotto: cooked.
Crostino: a crouton, or small piece of bread toasted or fried.
Crudo: raw.
Dolce: sweet.
Dolci: sweets and cakes.
Dough: flour and water mixtures before cooking, often with butter, eggs or other ingredients added.
Fagioli: dried beans.
Fagiolini: fresh green string or French beans.
Flambé: describes food set alight with ignited brandy or spirits.
Formaggio: cheese.
Freddo: cold.
Fritto: fried.
Frutti di mare: a selection of 'fruits from the sea'—different kinds of seafood.
Gamberetti: small prawns.
Gamberi: prawns.
Garlic: one of the onion family. The bulb divides into several 'cloves', each in its own papery skin. Crush, chop or put through a garlic press to use in savoury dishes. It has very pungent onion flavour, so should be used cautiously.
Gelatine: a water-soluble leaf or powder which forms a clear tasteless jelly when set.
Gelato: ice cream.
Genoese sponge: a particular kind of very light cake. Eggs, and sugar are whisked together until thick, then flour is added to make a batter before cooking.
Gnocchi: dumplings.
Granita: Italian water-ice.
Imbottito: stuffed.
Infuse: to steep herbs, spices and flavourings in a very hot liquid until the flavour has been absorbed.
Insalata: salad.
Lumache: snails.
Marinato: marinated food, i.e., food steeped in a strong liquid of wine, vinegar or citrus juice with oil and flavourings for several hours, either before or after cooking.
Minestre: soup or pasta course.
Misto: mixture.
Pasta: flour and water dough, used to make many different and distinctive shapes.
Pasta all'uovo: pasta dough with eggs added to it before shaping.
Pasta asciutta: pasta served plain or with a sauce.
Pasta in brodo: pasta cooked and served in a broth.
Pasta verde: green pasta, which has spinach added to the dough.
Peperoni: green or sweet red peppers; also the name of a spiced pork sausage with peppers to flavour it.
Pesce: fish.
Pesto: paste of fresh basil, Parmesan, garlic and oil.
Pitted: with stone removed, i.e. of olives.
Pollo: chicken.
Reduce: to concentrate a liquid by boiling and evaporating.
Scampi: a variety of very large prawn. In the British Isles the best equivalent is Dublin bay prawns.
Secco: dry.
Simmer: to cook gently in a liquid from 85°-91° C (185°-195° F), just below boiling point. This prevents soft foods breaking up or uneven cooking of foods.
Tartufi: truffles, a rare mushroom-like fungus. It can be dark or light in colour and has a firm texture and very delicate flavour.
Tonno: tuna fish.
Torta: cake.
Yeast: fungus cells used to produce alchoholic fermentation or cause dough to rise.
Zest: coloured oily outer skin of citrus fruit covering the white bitter pith. Used to flavour foods and liquids.

Index

Credits

Artists
John Booth
Ron Hayward Art Group
Ilric Shetland
Yvonne Sloggett

Photographs
Collezione Agnesi: 7 (bottom)
J. Allan Cash: 13 (bottom)
Federico Garolla/Editoriale Gemini: 17 (top)
Guglielmo Mairani: contents, 18
Peter Myers: 23 (top), 24, 29, 33, 36, 40, 41, 48, 53, 56, 65, 68, 73, 80, 88-9
Pictor: 10, 11, 17 (bottom), 44
Scala: 5
Servizio Editoriale Fotografico: 16 (top), 19
Ronald Sheridan: 6, 7 (top)
John Sims: contents
Tessa Traeger: 13 (top), 20-21, 60, 76-7, 84-5
M. Delluc/VIVA: 14
William Klein/VIVA: contents, 15
ZEFA: cover background

Grateful thanks to Elizabeth David Ltd for the loan of china and kitchen equipment, and to Fratelli Camisa and Lina Stores of Soho for the loan of food for photography.

Picture research and styling: Jenny de Gex

Food preparation for the cookery photographs was by:
Gilly Cubitt: 29, 40, 73
Alex Dufort: 33, 36, 48, 53, 56, 65, 68, 76-7, 80, 84-5, 88-9
Dinah Morrison: 20-21, 60

Cover
Design: Barry Kemp
Photographed and arranged by Tessa Traeger